James Little

The tercentenary of England's great victory over Spain and the Armada, 1588-1888

James Little

The tercentenary of England's great victory over Spain and the Armada, 1588-1888

ISBN/EAN: 9783337229863

Printed in Europe, USA, Canada, Australia, Japan

Cover: Foto ©ninafisch / pixelio.de

More available books at **www.hansebooks.com**

THE
TERCENTENARY

OF

ENGLAND'S GREAT VICTORY

OVER

SPAIN AND THE ARMADA.

1588—1888.

By REV. JAMES LITTLE, M.A.

TORONTO, CANADA:
WILLIAM BRIGGS, 78 & 80 KING STREET EAST.
MONTREAL: C. W. COATES.   HALIFAX: S. F. HUESTIS
1888.

PREFACE.

Mr. Coleridge observes that there are three points which the writer of a book must settle in his preface, viz., to what sort his book belongs, for what description of readers it is intended, and what is the specific end it is to answer.

Accepting this view as satisfactory, my preface shall consist mainly of brief replies to these three inquiries.

In reference to the first point, I answer that my little book does not treat of Philosophy, Science or Theology, though it is not out of harmony with what is known in these high spheres of thought. Nor does it belong to the more popular, if less elevated, realm of thought—the biographical fiction, or historical romance. The sort to which it does belong, but of which it is merely a fragment, is the *historical*. It describes, however, an epoch of rare interest in the history of our Anglo-Saxon race and of human progress.

As to the description of persons for whom I intend the book, I answer—I offer it to all who love the religious and rational freedom, to all who cherish the traditions and memory, for all the descendants—natural or political—of the heroic fathers who in 1588 struggled against and conquered the despotism and intolerance of the Chief Priest and the Most Catholic King of Christendom, and won the heritage of freedom and independence which has fallen to their children. I intend it especially for the *young* of this large family, the great Anglo-Saxon household. To them 1588 was not only an era in their history, as a race, but in progress toward freedom of intelligence, of civil rights and of religion. The heirs of such an inheritance must not sink into supineness or indifference in regard to it, but must clearly recognize and firmly stand by and defend it, if possible, extending the blessings it brings to those who yet enjoy them not.

Then, as to the end the book seeks to promote, I answer— It is the enlightening, elevation and exaltation of men's aims, principles and character. It is the exaltation of patriotism and piety above material and present interests. To show the people of our time, as the struggle of 1588 so clearly does, that the victory of great principles, of human rights, of freedom in our relations to God and men, are better worthy of a struggle than the conquest of territory or the triumphs of material wealth or advantage.

I shall only add that I have carefully consulted the best authorities within my reach, both on the events directly belonging to my subject, and those contemporary with it. I have, as to some extent will be seen in the pages of the book, consulted or cited: "Hume's History of England,"—"Macaulay's Essays and Criticisms,"—"Camden's Annals of England,"—"Knight's History of England,"—Motley's volumes on "The Rise of the Dutch Republic," and on "The United Netherlands,"—"Froude's History of England,"—"Hallam's Constitutional History of England,"—"Green's History of the English People," both the larger and smaller works—"McFarlane's Pictorial History of England,"—"Macintosh's History of England,"—"Prescott's Ferdinand and Isabella," (for character of the Inquisition)—also, "Dr. McCrie's History of the Reformation in Spain,"—Church Histories of both Scotland and England, for the era. Besides collateral helps, such as "Aikens' Court and Times of Elizabeth,"—"Creighton's Age of Elizabeth," etc.

From one source the information is now more copious than thirty or forty years ago, *i.e.*, in regard to the Spanish side. The correspondence of Philip the Second and his cotemporaries, which was long kept concealed, has been made accessible in recent days, and has furnished much fuller knowledge of his character and of his age than was before enjoyed.

CONTENTS.

Chap.		Page.
I.	Annus Mirabilis	9
II.	Magnates on the Spanish Side	14
III.	Leaders on the English Side	24
IV.	The Causes and Motives of the Invasion	31
V.	Causes, Motives and Designs of the Invasion (*continued*)	37
VI.	The Armada	42
VII.	The Spanish Army	48
VIII.	Various Delays in the Sailing of the Armada	53
IX.	England's Danger	63
X.	England's Danger on the Papal Side	73
XI.	England's Danger, from a Military Point of View	84
XII.	England's Preparations for War—Naval and Military	93
XIII.	The King of Spain Prescribes the Plan of Movement	104
XIV.	The Struggle up the Channel	111
XV.	The Struggle off Calais	128
XVI.	The Battle of Gravelines	138
XVII.	The Shattered Armada Escaping by the North Sea	153

CONTENTS.

Chap.		Page.
XVIII.	The Political Effects of the Defeat on the King of Spain	170
XIX.	Joyful Thanksgiving in England	179
XX.	The Character of the Victory	186
XXI.	Effects of the Victory on the Cause of Freedom	195
XXII.	Its Effects on England's National Life	200
XXIII.	Evidences of the Ruling of a Divine Hand	209
XXIV.	Our Heritage should be Preserved	217
XXV.	A Lesson from the Fathers of 1588 to their Canadian Children	227

1588

OR

THE TERCENTENARY OF ENGLAND'S GREAT VICTORY

OVER

SPAIN AND THE INVINCIBLE ARMADA.

CHAPTER I.

ANNUS MIRABILIS.

"Our fathers have told us what works thou didst in their days, in the times of old."—DAVID.

1588 Conspicuous in the annals of English history.

AMONG the years memorable in English history, fifteen hundred and eighty-eight will long hold, on many accounts, a conspicuous place. In that year England began to illustrate such latent powers, imperial

England's future greatness then foreshadowed.

courage and superior skill in naval warfare, that she soon successfully asserted her right to be styled mistress of the seas, an honour hitherto enjoyed by Spain. Also, in the promptness with which she organized, from crude and undisciplined materials, a numerous and patriotic army of defence, she proclaimed her love of queen and country, of home and altar, as well as her purpose to defend them against all invaders. The best of her people gave no less decisive proof of settled purpose to maintain the principles of political and religious liberty and independence than they had given of sincerity in receiving and openly professing them. We especially cherish an undying and grateful admiration of the heroic resistance offered by the patriotic English fathers of that day to the superior power of Spain, which menaced their country with invasion and conquest. The writer wishes, while the Tercentenary of England's glorious victory over the "Invincible Armada," and the proud hosts of Catholic Spain, is being celebrated, to contribute his mite in its honour. He proposes, with this intent, to give his best efforts to impartially relating once again the often, but not too often, told story of the scenes and incidents of the contest of that *annus mirabilis*. He proposes telling how British freemen, full of British

[margin notes: Undying admiration due the patriotic fathers of 1588. The occasion of this writing the observance of the Tercentenary of the scenes and incidents of 1588.]

How British valor triumphed over the superior power of intolerance.

valour, though comparatively few in number, and of limited resources, by the favour of Providence won a complete victory over the immense, well-disciplined and organized forces of Spain. Also, how they defeated and brought to naught a complicated and dangerous plot for the subjugation of their civil rights to Spain

How the plot was overthrown and the vanquished became as chaff before the wind.

and their religious freedom to Rome ; and how the veteran army of the invaders and their proud Armada were broken to pieces, and became like chaff before the winds. While England and her Low Country allies, together with the reformed religion, were preserved from perishing, as was threatened, by the hand of the bigoted King of Spain and the arts of the "Holy In-

The good resulting to human liberty and religious toleration.

quisition." It will further be seen how the mustard-seed of Christian freedom, then sown in the good soil of the Anglo-Saxon race, has become a great tree, under whose shadow and in whose branches the oppressed of every nation find shelter.

We wish to preserve the memory of those heroic sires who won the inheritance.

We who inherit the blessed fruits and results of that unequal struggle, owe the memory of those heroic sires by whom they were so nobly and successfully achieved, the tribute of a loving remembrance and appreciative mention, that their honoured names and deeds may never fade or perish from the memory of their children. We also owe it to the young of our own generation that we make known to them the historical traditions and remains which point out the way by which the great race and national heritage we enjoy was secured and won. Then may they in turn tell it to the generation following, and so "the unborn may arise and tell the same to their children."

We tell our generation, and they those who follow.

Besides, it tends to inspire our own patriotism, fill us with wholesome admiration and love of the powerful agents, human and divine, which secured them, and arouses manly purposes in us to preserve and defend them for those who shall come after us. The Greek historian, never tired writing, the bard singing, or the orator speaking of the heroic deeds of their fathers at Salamis, Actium, Marathon or Thermopylæ. Nor did the sacred historian, prophet or poet ever cease or weary relating in the loftiest forms of Hebrew eloquence the grand and majestic doings of their fathers and their fathers' God in Egypt, at the Red Sea, in the wilderness, at the Jordan, and in the conquest of the Land of Canaan.

Recalling the fathers inspires us.

The Greeks celebrated the heroic deeds of their fathers.

So did the Hebrews.

We should keep alive the memory of, and celebrate the great achievements of the past.

Why should not the memory of the noble struggle and glorious victory of our English fleet over the despot of Spain, and his defiant Armada, be kept in perpetual remembrance? Why should not we, who enjoy the rich and enduring fruits of the freedom, enterprise, and independence then achieved, write, speak, or sing, as we can, of the heroic deeds by which they have been won? Or why should this Tercentenary year pass by uncelebrated in Canada, whose civilization is a shoot of the old Anglo-Saxon stock, which not only conquered the Spanish invader, but which secured, and has preserved for their posterity, all that gives vitality, beneficence and endurance to our civilization? For the victory of 1588 was not merely that of England over the power of Spain, but of liberty over despotism, of Protestantism over Popery, of modern life and progress over mediævalism.

First introduce the chief personages of the drama.

Before proceeding to relate the causes, motives, and designs of the Spanish invasion of England, we will introduce to our readers the principal personages who acted in, brought on, or directed the drama of that bold enterprise.

CHAPTER II.

MAGNATES ON THE SPANISH SIDE.

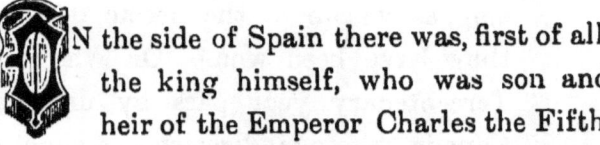

First, the King of Spain himself.

ON the side of Spain there was, first of all, the king himself, who was son and heir of the Emperor Charles the Fifth. On the morning of almost any day in the spring of 1588, there might be seen entering a cabinet in the palace of the Escorial* a man of short stature, narrow chest, spindling legs and meagre physique. His hair was gray and close cut, his

---

* The Escorial, or Escurial, was a magnificent pile of buildings erected by Philip the Second on an elevated and lonely plateau in the very centre of Spain, some twenty-seven miles west of Madrid. It was undertaken soon after the battle of St. Quentin (in 1557), and was nearly twenty years in course of erection. It was designed for the triple purpose of a palace, a fortress, and a convent. The pile was erected in honor of St. Lawrence, on whose day the victorious battle of St. Quentin was fought with France, and to whom Philip ascribed his victory. That saint had suffered martyrdom, as it will be remembered, by being roasted on a gridiron, and hence the peculiar form of the Escurial, which is after the pattern of the saint's instrument of torture.

ENGLAND'S VICTORY OVER THE ARMADA

His personal appearance.

eyes a blue-gray, his forehead wide, his nose long and crooked, his mouth wide and his lower jaw heavy and protruding. His look was cold, distant and severe. The expression of his countenance was haughty, ungenial and almost sullen.

Ungenial, distant and silent.

His bearing and manner were timid, mean and taciturn. It may be added that his soul was dark and gloomy, as his face was dreary. Such was the personal appearance of Philip* the Second, King of Spain, as he entered the office at which he laboured daily seven or eight hours.

A plodding worker at his desk.

For he was most assiduous in prosecuting the work of his desk. He never ceased for a moment during these hours, issuing, correcting or signing despatches to or from different parts of his vast dominions. Thus by his pen, and according to his own good pleasure, he governed the largest and most powerful kingdom of Christendom. His power was absolute. His will,

Absolute and despotic in his government.

---

* Philip the Second was born in Spain in May, 1527. In 1543 he married his cousin Maria of Portugal, who lived thereafter only one year. In 1554 he again entered the married state, having selected for his wife, Mary Tudor, Queen of England. In 1555, on the abdication of his father, he assumed the sovereignty of Spain and all its dependencies. Philip was, therefore, in the sixty-second year of his age, and thirty-third of his reign, at the date of the invasion of England.

even his whims, was observed and obeyed. No one dare challenge any of his deeds, or ask a reason for his most arbitrary and intolerant exercise of power. He claimed the power of life and death over all his subjects. He proclaimed war or made peace without consulting any of his nobles, rulers or people. Their substance—houses and estates, as well as money and goods—he regarded as his, even as the people themselves belonged to him. His jurisdiction over their religious convictions and beliefs he claimed to be supreme. He appointed or removed ministers of state, judges, admirals, generals, bishops, and all the rest, not on the grounds of merit or demerit, but according to his own will. It might be said of him as Daniel said of Nebuchadnezzar, the despot of Babylon, that God had given him a "kingdom" and "majesty," and that his people of "every nation and language trembled and feared before him; whom he would he slew; and whom he would he kept alive; and whom he would he set up, and whom he would he put down."

Philip exercised absolute power over the people's lives, property, etc.

Absolute as the despot of Babylon.

Not a man of words but of the pen.
He did all his work with his pen, doing nothing with his tongue or with his sword. He never thought of taking the field on great

occasions, as his father delighted to do. He seldom used many words; never any if he could help it. He would rather scrawl a dozen pages than make an oral reply in either of the monosyllables, yes or no. His mind was narrow and torpid, rather than comprehensive or vigorous. It had never been expanded by liberal culture. His education was limited, and derived chiefly from monks, priests and inquisitors. He was a pampered child of full years. He never became a well-rounded and solidly reasoning man. He knew no language but the Spanish, associated with none but Spaniards, carried on his government almost exclusively by Spaniards. He had in spirit, as he inherited by birth, all the pride, exclusiveness and intolerance of a genuine Spaniard. But he was a Spaniard above all in zeal for the papal religion, and hatred of all other forms of belief. He had, on succeeding to power in 1555, consciously and resolutely devoted himself, his life, resources and kingly power, to maintain the Catholic religion and to destroy heresy and heretics in every part of his dominions. This was the one aim of his life, from which he never shrunk. He was as regular as a monk in

Narrow minded and imperfectly educated.

Only a Spaniard and nothing more.

Devoted himself to maintain the papal religion.

Punctual in observing the ritual of his religion.

observing the requirements of the Romish ritual. He attended mass, prayers and vespers daily. Listened patiently to frequent exhortations on religion, submitted his conscience to the inspection of his confessor, and had all the needs of his soul regularly attended to by a duly authorized staff of spiritual health officers. These things attended to, he felt at liberty to

No scruple as to self-indulgence or the rights of his neighbours.

indulge in such carnal pleasures as he chose, to excite wars among neighbouring states, bring under his sceptre such as were too weak to resist him, or, by means of the Inquisition, to burn alive, torture or imprison, Moslems, Jews, or Protestants who would not, like himself, believe that salvation could be found only in the Church of Rome.

"The Holy Inquisition, thoroughly established as it was in his ancestral Spain, was a portion of the regular working machinery by which his absolute kingship and his superhuman will expressed themselves. A tribunal which performed its functions with a celerity, certainty and irresistibility resembling the attributes of Omnipotence; which, like the pestilence, entered palace or hovel at will, and which smote the wretch guilty or suspected of heresy with a precision against which no human ingenuity or sympathy could guard—such an institution could not but be dear to his heart. It was inevitable that the extension and perpetuation of what he deemed its blessings throughout his dominions, should be his settled purpose. Spain was governed by an established terrorism. The Grand Inquisitor was almost as awful a personage as the king or the pope. His familiars were in every village and at every fireside, and from their fangs there was no escape. Millions of Spaniards would have rebelled against the Crown or accepted the reformed religion, had they not been perfectly certain of being burned or hanged at the slightest movement in such a direction."*

Extent of Philip's possessions. The kingdom of Philip—*the Most Catholic King*, as he delighted to be called—excelled any in Europe during his day in wealth, population and power. It included the whole of the Spanish peninsula, *i.e.*, Castile, Aragon, Granada and Portugal; in Italy, the Two Sicilies, Naples and the Duchy of Milan; in the Low Countries, the Dukedom of Burgundy and sev-

---

* United Netherlands, Vol. 2.

enteen Netherland provinces. He was also sovereign of all the Americas, lord of Asia and Africa, and titular king of Jerusalem, France and England. Lord Macaulay says of his power: "During the greater part of his reign Philip was supreme on both elements. His soldiers marched up to the capital of France, his ships menaced the shores of England. It was no exaggeration to say that during several years his power over Europe was greater than even that of Napoleon."

Macaulay's estimate of his power.

We may add the acknowledged fact that the Spanish infantry were the most renowned, while the Spanish generals were unrivalled in Europe. These, with the vast resources of the Spanish dominions, were under the control of one will, and that the king's.

The king had, in 1588, two principal advisers attached to his cabinet, who were, however, merely his private secretaries. The one was Don Juan de Idiaquez, who was called Chief Secretary of State and War. The other was Don Cristoval de Moura, head of the Department of Finance and of the Administration of Portugal and Castile. This latter was the king's chief favourite or attendant.

His two secretaries, Idiaquez and Moura.

Neither of these men, though both were able and cultured, was a responsible minister. The king, their master, assumed all responsibility. Their duty was to elaborate and put in due form all despatches and state papers after the king had intimated his will or given his orders. When they had reduced the crude materials of the king's orders into proper form, he scrawled his corrections and added his signature, so giving them authority. Great, diligent and arduous as were their labours, and even high their rank, their names seldom come to notice in the history of the time.

Next to the king in giving effect to the scheme of the invasion was his general and chief in the Netherlands, Alexander Farnese, Duke of Parma, then in the forty-third year of his age. Farnese was a man of rare gifts and great talents. He was astute, sagacious, intrepid, full of resources, and of immense energy. To him alone, of all outside his cabinet, the king confided the plot of the invasion, and took counsel concerning the means whereby it was to be carried into effect.

Another distinguished name and ally on the Spanish side was Pope Sixtus the Fifth. He was of humble origin, had been brought up in a monastery, and bore himself with assumed humility and gentleness, while yet his heart was full of pride, ambition and eagerness for family aggrandizement. He warmly approved and earnestly urged Philip's enterprise. He gave all force to the thunderbolts of excommunication already hurled at the heads of all the Protestant princes of Christendom—against William of Orange or William the Silent, King Henry of Navarre, as against the Queen of England. For by these means he both hoped to receive new honours and dignity for his relatives, and to bring the countries over which these princes exercised power, to submit to the papal see. He, therefore, offered King Philip stimulating arguments in words and money to help on the scheme of the invasion of England. It is true His Holiness loved money, and only after long bargaining with Philip promised to give one million gold ducats to the great enterprise. For by it, above everything else, he was confident he would be enabled to strike down heresy in England, and restore her to the ancient faith.

Marginalia:
- Assumed humility, of great pride and ambition.
- Thunderbolts of excommunication hurled at all Protestant princes.
- Pope promises one million gold ducats.

The Marquis of Santa Crux Captain-general of the Armada.

There was besides, the Marquis of Santa Crux, to whom the king first assigned the work of preparing and organizing the Armada, and then appointed him Captain-general of the whole Armada. The marquis was a naval officer of the highest distinction and long experience in the king's service. He had the rare good fortune of having never lost a battle or sustained a defeat during thirty years of public service. He had now to co-operate in

Of great experience and ability.

the business of the invasion with the Duke of Parma, for whom he entertained no cordial affection. The duke reciprocated the like feelings. Unfortunately for the marquis, neither had his master, the king, any cordiality nor even kindness of feeling toward him. Indeed,

Illtreated by his master.

he treated his greatest sea-captain with coldness, and paid little attention to any of his wishes or suggestions. This crippled his efforts and chilled his zeal in preparing for the expedition. He did not, as we shall by-and-by see, command the expedition, but was succeeded by the rich Duke of Medina Sidonia, who, happily for England, knew less of naval warfare than his predecessor.

CHAPTER III.

LEADERS ON THE ENGLISH SIDE.

Queen Elizabeth.

AMONG the English chiefs, the first name in prominence and importance is Elizabeth Tudor, Queen of England.

Was fifty-five at the time of the invasion.

When she ascended the throne in 1558 she was twenty-five years of age. She was, consequently, fifty-five when the invasion took place. She

Her personal appearance and character.

was still in the vigour of mature and buoyant life. Elizabeth had a commanding presence, a clear understanding, a strong will and bright countenance; but possessed a violent temper, a strong self-will, an arbitrary spirit, and was liable to fits of jealousy as well toward women as men. She had a quick discernment of the character and talents of men, and always

Good judgment in selecting ministers.

selected with good judgment her ministers and officers of state. It must also be said she was not free from that deceit and craft which, in her day, were regarded by princes as a becoming qualification and a rightful heritage. Her personal appearance and manners were pleasing and vivacious, though she was not a model of grace or beauty. Her complexion was fair, her hair almost red, her nose rather long and crooked, her eyes small and bright. The lines of her face were strongly marked and rather masculine. Dickens says, "she was rather a hard swearer, and coarse talker." She loved to exercise absolute power. She magnified her prerogative, and bore with unsparing severity on any one who infringed upon its sacred rights.

Vivacious and pleasing, not beautiful.

Hot temper, coarse in speech.

After all, however, we must admit that she was a woman of superior capacity, judgment and spirit, a successful ruler and a great queen. If she was imperious, she was politic; if intolerant, she was considerate; if passionate, she was firm in her purpose and persistent in its accomplishment. If strict in the exaction of money, she was prudent, even economical, in the use of it. It should also be remembered that she spent both her money and her life in promoting the well-being of her country, which she greatly loved.*

A great queen and true patriot.

---

* "Elizabeth was more exacting," says Macaulay, "of the homage of her subjects than Louis XIV., but, unlike

England's population less than four and a half millions

At that time, and during the reign of Elizabeth, the population of England did not reach quite four and a half million souls.* That is to say, it did not quite equal the present population of London, the capital of the empire; and was about equal to that of our Dominion in this Tercentenary year. The revenue of the queen, for stinginess in the use of which she is often severely blamed, was not one-hundredth part of England's present revenue.

The queen's revenue only one-half million sterling.

Lord Macaulay makes this remark when comparing it with that of her great adversary, Philip of Spain. He says, "His annual revenue amounted in the season of his greatest prosperity to four millions sterling, or eight times as large as that which England yielded to Elizabeth." He might have gone much higher in estimating Philip's revenues. They reached fourteen millions for many years.

---

him or Philip of Spain, she had no power to enforce it. Hers was simply the popular deference paid to the office; to the ancient line in which it resided and in the sense of security enjoyed by the people. The English people of the sixteenth century were free, though they had not the witnessed forms nor present modes of asserting it."

* Hallam's Const. History of England.

There are English gentlemen who now think themselves hardly pressed to meet their personal and private expenses, whose incomes are yet larger than that on which the Queen of England maintained her royal state. The population of London in that day was about one hundred and fifty thousand, which, our readers will observe, is little more than the estimated population of our own city of Toronto at the present time.

Some English gentlemen spend more than did the queen.

London in 1588 had only 150,000 population.

Next after the queen we may mention the name of Robert Dudley, Earl of Leicester—a gallant courtier, an enterprising general, and chosen favourite of the queen, to whom she entrusted the chief command of her army at the crisis of the invasion. Leicester, though ambitious, and inclined to be vainglorious, yet freely spent his fortune and talents in the queen's service, and on behalf of his country and of liberty.

The Earl of Leicester.

There was also the accomplished and brilliant young nobleman, Robert Devereux, Earl of Essex, whose career closed both unhappily and early. He was younger by a whole generation than Leicester, yet, after the latter's death, he became the queen's special favourite

The Earl of Essex.

in her most capricious days—a distinction which proved fatal, though for the time tending to his promotion. He did most gallant service for his queen in the present crisis.

The queen had long experience in the government of England at the date of the Spanish invasion. She had the aid of many singularly wise, able and patriotic statesmen. First, she had Lord Burleigh, the minister who so wisely and successfully directed public affairs at the time of her accession, and who was then known as Sir William Cecil. In his green old age he was still able to do valuable work, and give prudent counsel. For he knew the resources, temper and peculiarities of the nation better than any statesman of the realm, as well as how to adjust and harmonize their often conflicting forces.

Lord Burleigh, erewhile Sir William Cecil.

Her present chief minister and adviser was Sir Francis Walshingham—a man of high character, an indefatigable worker, a quick discerner of men's schemes and plots, capable, patriotic, and every way worthy of the great trust reposed in him. No monarch ever had a more conscientious, vigilant, sagacious and upright minister, or one better suited to the

Sir Francis Walshingham, First Minister of Elizabeth.

times. His almost infallible detection of treasonable plots and schemes more than once saved the queen's life.

Sir Walter Raleigh.

Sir Walter Raleigh, somewhile the queen's favourite, filled many posts of public usefulness. He was gifted with a rare versatility of talent. He could command an army or a fleet, write a book or grace the court of his sovereign, scour the high seas, or plant colonies in America, all of which works and positions he had, one time or another, performed and filled. He had recently returned from a rather unsuccessful attempt at colonizing those parts of America on the Roanoke which are now included in Virginia and North Carolina. This bold spirit,

He and other patriots rally to the defence of their country.

like so many distinguished and patriotic gentlemen and sea-captains, rallied to his country's defence when the note of her invasion by the intolerant Spaniard was sounded.

Lord Howard.

Lord Howard of Effingham—a brave and genial peer—was by the queen appointed Lord Admiral of England, and to him she entrusted the command of her navy. Sir

Sir Francis Drake.

Francis Drake—who was the first Englishman to circumnavigate the globe, and who had, by his bold deeds upon the high seas, made his name a terror to the King of Spain—was appointed vice-admiral of the English fleet. The

Frobisher. intrepid and gallant Captain Frobisher, who had three times penetrated the polar seas, commanded the largest ship in the queen's navy.

Hawkins. The courageous Hawkins, who had sailed two oceans, captured many prizes, and made the name of English seamen a terror to their enemies, was rear-admiral. Among the other bold seamen whose names are remembered is that of

Cavendish. Cavendish, who, in the beginning of 1588, was on the Pacific Ocean despoiling Philip's galleons off the coasts of Chili and California. Also, Lord Thomas Seymour, Sir William Winter and many others were conspicuous for gallantry and patriotism.

Besides such statesmen, sea-captains and soldiers, England was in that age illustrated in

Bacon, Spencer, and Shakespeare. the realms of thought and letters by the genius of Bacon, Spencer and Shakespeare—names sufficient to throw an undying lustre on any age.

CHAPTER IV.

THE CAUSES AND MOTIVES OF THE INVASION.

<small>The contention originated in ideas which the Reformation introduced into men's minds.</small>

THESE must be traced to and found in that greatest religious and social movement of the century—the Reformation. New light had entered men's minds, not only in regard to the means by which we enjoy the divine favour and are made heirs of heaven, but also as to our rights and privileges as citizens of the state and members of the church. A new standard of faith and rules of conduct had been found. The question was not now what the pope, the clergy or the church commanded, but what the Scriptures, the Word of God, commanded. The authority of this new rule quite cast out that of the old. In the light

<small>The authority of the Scriptures preferred to the pope's.</small>

and by the authority of Scripture the minds of men were emancipated from the tyranny of those who called themselves the church and claimed to sway all the power of heaven and earth. The multitudes whose souls were filled with these new views, and who felt these new convictions, could not but cherish and affirm them. They were so real, so evident and so blessed, they could not surrender them. In preference, they gladly renounced the papal authority and withdrew from the Church of Rome. The papacy, which then, as now, claimed supremacy over both state and church—over both the conscience and conduct of men—stirred all her power, employed all her arts to allure, persuade, or coerce all dissentients to return to Rome and acknowledge and obey the pope. In the great rational and spiritual awakening—in the refreshing and reinvigoration of the era—some of the nations of Europe shared very largely; others, though roused and agitated by, did not receive or adopt, the Reformation. Some obstinately rejected and resisted its beneficent influence. "Before all others Spain strove fiercely to extinguish its very life." Like Gideon's fleece, says an eloquent writer, "when all around was wet with the dews of heaven, Spain alone remained dry."

The latter renounced.

Spain historically and obstinately intolerant.

Before the Reformation had extended itself in Christendom, as early as the days of the conquests of Ferdinand and Isabella, that kingdom put in motion that cruel and murderous machine, "the Holy Office of the Inquisition." By it she had burnt alive, tortured, imprisoned, enslaved or exiled tens of thousands of unoffending Moslems and Jews. When she desired spoils or sought revenge on those hapless people, she first branded them with the odious name, *Infidel*, then in the spirit, not of the Christ, but of His enemy, she destroyed their lives, refusing to save them.

A new and fruitful field opened before this merciless instrument of Spanish despotism when the Reformation began to draw away many of those who before belonged to the established church. In her bigotry and pride Spain claimed and exercised a monopoly of papal zeal, and was known and acknowledged as the most devoted nation of Europe in the maintenance of the papacy, and relentless opposition to every form of dissent.

Exercises despotism over right of thought and of belief.

The Spanish Inquisition destroyed multitudes of Moors and Jews.

The Reformation opened a new field for the Inquisition.

"The Inquisition had a fatally perfect organization throughout her territory. It was sustained by all the power of the Crown. It had its spies among the *familiars*, who entered

The familiars, Jesuits and Dominicans, work the machine.

every home and presumed to know even the thoughts of every heart. It had its inquisitors and executioners among the Jesuits and Dominicans, who laid relentless hands on all suspected of heresy, and with iron grasp held them till they had expiated the crimes with which they were accused, with torture, exile or their blood.

In the Netherlands 100,000 fell by the Inquisition from 1521-1555.

In the Netherlands, which were included in Philip's dominions, the Inquisition had been set up by Charles V. From the beginning of the Reformation to the abdication of Charles in 1555, we are informed on excellent authority that "there were burned, strangled, beheaded or buried alive for such offences as reading the Scriptures, looking askance at a graven image, or ridiculing the actual presence of the body and blood of Christ in a wafer, not less than a hundred thousand persons."*

The effects of this instrument on Spain, Italy, etc.

The terror of the Inquisition paralyzed, almost extinguished, the young life of the Reformation in Spain, Italy, and parts of Germany. So closely did its minions watch, so quickly swoop down upon, and so relentlessly punish, all who accepted, favoured, or were suspected of favouring the reformed religion, that few were left who dare own the odious heresy. To such state of feeling did the devotees of the

---

*Motley.

SOLEIMAN THE MAGNIFICENT

Inquisition strive to bring the people, that they would regard the reformed religion as a plague or pestilence, which required for the safety of the well that those infected should be cut off from among them. It added to the horror to be assured that the hopeless heretic was excluded as well from all the bliss of the life to come.

Led to revolt in the Netherlands.

The introduction of this liberty-destroying, conscience-stultifying institution into the Netherlands aroused the people to rebellion, and led to a terrible war which lasted for eighty years.

The two despots, the King of Spain and the Pope of Rome conspire to crush liberty and human rights.

The royal and sacerdotal despots, the King of Spain and the Pope of Rome, were united in purpose to extinguish the very spirit of freedom, to put a perpetual end to liberty of conscience, and to silence every aspiration of individualism. "Men in the mass and men severally must obey the powers God has placed over them," said the monarch and the chief priest. They added, "men must not qualify or condition this obedience; for God speaks in and through His anointed kings and priests." In Protestant England and Holland, the monarch and the minister of God were loved and honoured; but the people had rights and privileges which were also acknowledged and respected. There were

Protestantism had the germs, not yet the developed thing.

Toleration slowly but surely reached.

limits and conditions both to authority and obedience. These were not then indeed very clearly defined or well understood; for Queen Elizabeth was almost as absolute in spirit as Philip; and the Protestant churches had not yet learned to practise toleration. There were, however, great principles—germs of liberty, acknowledged, which served in that day; but which, after many years of bitter struggle, were developed into and reached a blessed completeness and maturity.

CHAPTER V.

CAUSES, MOTIVES AND DESIGNS OF THE INVASION (CONTINUED).

Philip's bigoted and persecuting spirit and purpose.

THE object which the King of Spain set before himself on ascending the throne of his kingdom was first, and above everything else, to destroy heresy and defend the ancient, and orthodox, which was, of course, the Romish, Church. He gloried in this more even than in enlarging his dominions, or swaying a beneficent sceptre over the millions who acknowledged it.

His persecutions in the Netherlands.

In 1559, nearly four years after assuming supreme power, when about taking leave of his subjects in the Low Country to return to his capital in Spain, and at the close of a general pacification, the royal bigot, in fierce and angry tones, denounced the heretical tendencies of the provinces, and gave peremptory orders for the summary execution of all heresy and heretics, requiring that "they be burnt, strangled or buried alive, without respect of persons, according to the edicts already in their hands, that so no vestige of heresy might be left."

Philip had long desired, but delayed, to strike England, because she was a check on France, which was ready to co-operate with his rebellious Netherland provinces; and because he feared she might, through her Scotch connections, gain mastery of England. This would have barred his own aspirations to the sovereignty of that country.

England an ally of the Low Countries against Philip's persecutions.

England had for several years given aid and comfort to the Low Countries, in their heroic struggle for freedom against the despotic power of Spain. She had aided them with her alliance, with her money, her soldiers and her navy. But for this help the cause of liberty and Protestantism would then have been crushed. With England's good will, however, the provinces were able to maintain a long and resolute struggle. At length Philip came to the conclusion that he could not destroy Protestantism in the provinces and re-establish the papacy unless he first humbled England. But Philip's anger was kindled against England, not only because she had given encouragement and help to his Low Country subjects who were in rebellion against him, and who wearied him with their persistent clamour about their liberties, their rights of religion and worship, which was nothing else than the plague-spot of heresy; but for her sins against his supremacy on the seas. Despite the papal decree which gave and made over the new world to him, England's ships had crossed the ocean, entered the waters of the West Indies, traversed the coasts of Chili and Peru, in the Pacific Ocean, had despoiled his galleons of their precious cargoes of gold dust and of the ingots of Potosi, of pearls, diamonds and precious stones from Lima. These ships on returning to England, after so much freebooting on seas which were his own, were not only not called to a reckoning for their piratical conduct, but were welcomed by her majesty as though conquerors. Francis Drake, their leader, was the son of a Kentish vicar, and was himself a Calvinist; yet had the queen knighted him, received a share of his booty and even placed, some of the gems he presented her, in her crown.

England was the vital and directing head, of

Protestantism. If he could crush England, it must fall. Besides, he greatly desired to rule the people he hoped to subdue. He believed by collecting a vast army, and concentrating his resources and his money on a navy, he could send such a force against England as would conquer her at a single stroke. Then his great life-work would speedily reach a happy realization. Protestantism would be swept away, and the ancient church be restored. His own dominions also would be widened, and would have rest from sectarian strife.

<small>Philip's reasonings on the good gained to him and the church by the overthrow of England.</small>

The head of the church was one with him in heart and unscrupulousness of purpose. No matter what wrong was done to men's rights, to conscience, to human progress, to the ages to come, neither of these hoary-headed and intolerant bigots either cared or acknowledged responsibility. The religious king is ready to use his vast earthly revenues to set up a kingdom of which its Founder said, "it is not of this world." The worldly priest is ready to use the boundless resources of his spiritual kingdom, its maledictions and benedictions, to pull down one and set up another temporal dominion. Day and night King Philip muses over his great enter-

<small>Disregard of the rights or wishes of men, or of the age.</small>

Philip's in-decision.

prise in the Escorial. He fears to decide upon it, though he longs for the results he imagines will certainly flow from it. It will require vast resources and preparations—provisions, ships, munitions, money and men. He writes to his favourite general, the Duke of Parma, in the Low Provinces, and asks his views. He waits, and hesitates in taking decisive action. Even when preparations begin to be made, he thinks they may be directed to the Indies or the con-quest of another province. When challenged by foreign ministers as to the design of these large preparations now going on, he dissembles and evades the inquiry. He does not openly acknowledge his designs until his fleet is almost ready for sea. Then he regards it as a power so mighty and irresistible that he spreads abroad its fame and magnifies its power, that he may strike terror into the hearts of the English, and break down their courage and humble their spirits before he has struck a blow. It is needless to say it had no such effects on them either first or last.

He evades an answer to the inquiry, "For what does he prepare"?

When the Armada is prepared, the king magnifies its power, and hopes to terrify England.

CHAPTER VI.

THE ARMADA.

The preparation of the Armada.

THE Armada provided for the invasion of England comprised the naval strength of Spain, and was provided by the gold which, of late years, had flowed into the nation's coffers from the East and West

The means derived from conquests.

Indies, and from the conquests and mines of Mexico and Peru. The shipyards of all the principal ports of Sicily, Naples, Spain and Portugal constantly resounded for over three years with the ring of shipbuilding and the

The place of rendezvous Lisbon on the Tagus.

bustle of preparation for war. The great rendezvous toward which all vessels, war-ships, transports, tenders, etc., moved, and in which all stores, munitions, provisions, soldiers, sutlers, etc., gathered, was Lisbon on the Tagus. There, during fifteen eighty-six, seven and eight, were collected great galleons, galeases and galleys, together with squadrons of smaller ships, from

ENGLAND'S VICTORY OVER THE ARMADA. 43

Biscay, Andalusia, Guiposcoa, as well as Castile, Sicily, Naples and Portugal.

<small>The number of ships in the Armada.</small>
The fleet of the Armada consisted of one hundred and thirty-four ships, of which nearly one hundred were galleons, galeases and galleys—ships of the largest size.

<small>The form and appearance of the largest.</small>
The galleons, about sixty in number, were huge, wide oval-shaped structures. Their bulwarks were very heavy, being three to four feet in thickness. Each was built up both fore and aft, prow and stern, in the form of a castle, in which were various rooms for the service of the ship. Between those castles the sides curved down to near the water's edge at midships. The galeases were considerably larger than the galleons. Each had one castellated fortress at the stern, and another, a little smaller, at the bows. Between these were the seats of the rowers, who were galley slaves, about three hundred in number on each ship.

<small>Rooms of state, chapels, etc.</small>
In the fortress, which in some cases was shot proof, were rooms of state, oratorys and chapels for worship, pulpits, gilded saints, madonnas, and bands of music. The galleys resembled in almost every respect those just described, but were somewhat smaller. These

large vessels were grand for spectacular imposingness and for effect, as every writer who has described them has observed. Nothing could have exceeded the Spanish fleet in this respect. But for war purposes, and for successfully navigating stormy seas nothing worse in the line of shipbuilding was ever constructed. They were too high and heavy above for their depth and draught below. Little or no canvas dared be spread on them in ordinary weather; but when storms prevailed they could not be managed, as they refused to obey either rudder or sail. Besides, they formed fine targets for their enemies, whose guns could hardly miss them, while the range of their own generally fell far over the heads of their enemies. Ships of such bulk, build and arrangement had never before been used in European warfare. The whole fleet was divided into ten squadrons. There was the squadron of Portugal, of Castile, of Andalusia, of Biscay, of Guiposcoa, of Italy, of Urcas, and four smaller squadrons.

Ill constructed for storms.

Fine targets.

Too high in their range to strike their enemies.

Ten squadrons in all.

The Captain-General the Duke of Medina Sidonia.
Vice-Admiral de Leyva.

The squadron of Portugal was in immediate command of the Duke of Medina Sidonia, Captain-General of the Armada. The Vice-Admiral was Don Alonzo de Leyva. The fleet was worked by eight thousand seven hundred and forty-six (8,746) sailors, and two thousand and eighty-eight (2,088) galley slaves. It was armed with three thousand one hundred and sixty-five (3,165) pieces of cannon, and carried over twenty thousand soldiers, and had a tonnage of about sixty thousand tons (60,000). There was, besides, some twenty lighter ships called caravels, each having ten slaves and six oars, attending the fleet. Every ship had "two boat loads of stones to throw in the time of fight, and wildfire to be given out to the most expert." There was also a gallant force of volunteers, some two thousand strong, most of them ambitious members of the most noble families of Spain, Portugal and Italy. There were Don John de Medici, Don Amadeus de Sevoi, and the Dukes of Savionetta and Pastronia, all eager for the great enterprise, and confident of its speedy success.

There was on board also a large contingent of Jesuits, friars and priests, who were to be spiritual guides to the soldiers, and to labour as missionaries in the conversion of England when the people were vanquished. Chief and head of all this spiritual force was Don Martin Alac-

Instruments of torture.

con, administrator of the Inquisition. He had with him, it is said, a plentiful supply of those pointed arguments — neck-stretchers, pincers, thumb-screws, and all such instruments as humble the proud, and dispose hard-hearted persons to sorrow, if not repentance.

Popish books.

He also had a large store of mass books, manuals of matins and vespers, a good many relics and bones of dead saints, and plenty of rosaries. He had, besides, a foul and libellous book, entitled, "An admonition to the nobility and people of England and Ireland, concerning the present war, made for the execution of his holiness' sentence, by the high and mighty King Catholic of Spain." It was signed Allen,

Character of this book against the queen.

Cardinal of England. This book, which was an insult to the whole nation, charged the foulest slanders on the queen's birth, right to the throne, and on her character as a Christian. Its design was to alienate her Catholic subjects from the queen's person and absolve them from obligation to her, that so they might the more eagerly conspire to set up in England the authority of Philip and the pope. It served an opposite purpose.

The whole number of souls on board the Armada exceeded thirty thousand. On the eve of its departure the Armada was duly blessed by Cardinal Archduke Albert, the viceroy of Portugal.

Thus the preparations were completed. They seemed sufficient for successfully carrying out the conspiracy of Philip and the pope against human liberty, *i.e.*, Protestantism : for the world's only hope of rational freedom at that day was bound up in the life of Protestantism. This immense war force now put in motion by the King of Spain and the Pope of Rome was the concrete embodiment of that king's most fixed purpose to crush out and subdue Protestantism, and bring the whole Christian world under the tyranny of the chief priest of Rome. It is pleasant to remember that—

> "Truth, crushed to earth, shall rise again;
> The eternal life of God is hers :
> But error, wounded, writhes in pain,
> And dies amid her worshippers."

[Marginal notes: The number of souls over 30,000. The Armada blessed. The whole force a conspiracy to perpetuate tyranny and destroy the rights of man.]

CHAPTER VII.

THE SPANISH ARMY.

A grand army collected in Flanders, commanded by the Duke of Parma.

A GRAND army was formed in Flanders of the Netherlands, which was to co-operate with the Armada in the invasion and conquest of England. It was in command of Alexander Farnese, Duke of Parma, the ablest general in the king's service. He was in the confidence of, and in sympathy with, his master in the whole enterprise. His army was largely composed of veterans who had distinguished themselves on many a field and in the siege of many a city of the Low Countries and of France. It was reinforced and recruited by adventurers of the lowest, as well as of the highest classes. There were courtiers of Italy, Spain and Portugal, as well as idlers, scapegraces and ne'er-do-wells of the Netherlands and different parts of Germany. The one class came in the name of religion and

The base and brave in it.

ENGLAND'S VICTORY OVER THE ARMADA. 49

for the glory of God, the other in the name of the king, and to obtain all the spoil they could secure. Both were, however, moved far more by the reputed wealth of England and the promise of being allowed freely to possess it as soon as England was conquered, than by either love or fear of God or of the king. Reinforcements poured into Parma's camp from all quarters of the Netherlands and Germany, as well as those just named. By the end of April (1588) the duke was in command of sixty thousand troops, supported at a monthly cost of about half a million crowns. Yet so rapid was the progress of disease, incident to crowded camps, and raw climate, that the number was sadly diminished before the time for employing services arrived.

Love of spoil.

The army reached 60,000 in April.

Rapidly diminished by disease.

[great] ambition sprang up among the ad[heren]ts of the King of Spain and followers of [the P]ope to crush, by a grand united effort, the [cause] of Protestantism, and so silence their [loud] cry for civil and religious liberty. The [utter] overthrow of England was confidently [predic]ted by them, and operated like the sound [of a] trumpet to arouse the Catholic world. [Scio]ns of royal houses, grandees of azure

Grandees rush to Farnese's camp.

blood, the bastard of Philip the Second, the bastard of Savoy, the bastard of Medina, the Archduke Charles, nephew of the emperor, the princes of Ascoli and Melfi, and many like them, together with such English traitors as Paget, Westmoreland and Stanley, all hurried to the camp of Farnese, as to some famous tournament in which it were a disgrace to chivalry if their names were not enrolled."*

Provision for the transportation of Parma's troops neglected by the king.

King Philip, who had a plodding but not a capacious or comprehensive mind, forgot the important matter of the means of transportation for the Duke of Parma's troops from Flanders to England. He had made no provision of ships or transports for this important part of the service. He forgot that, however brave and powerful Parma's troops might be, they could not conquer England if they remained at Ghent in Flanders. The duke, however,

The duke supplies the oversight by energy and great effort.

made prodigious efforts to provide the necessary means of transportation for his cavalry and infantry from Dunkirk, Newport, Gravelines, and the Scheldt to the Thames in England. He set all carpenters, shipbuilders and shipwrights of every kind which he was able

---

* U. N., p. 579.

to procure in Lower Germany, in Flanders or in the Baltic to build transports on all the rivers, canals and harbours through which he meant to pass. With incredible rapidity the Flemish forests were transformed, it was observed, into floating ships. But none of these vessels had any armament, nor were capable of resisting violent storms. They would serve, however, if the Armada should shield them all the way across the Channel, if no English ships and no adverse winds opposed. But how were they to get under the protection of the Armada? It could not go to them. They could not come to it, because an English fleet lay between. As matters turned out, they were strong, safe and sufficient. For none of them were ever used or found to be necessary.

The transports unarmed.

Parma's soldiers not provided with safe transportation.

This whole armament for the dethroning of Elizabeth, the conquest and conversion of England was a marvel to an age in which ships of twelve or thirteen hundred tons were seldom seen, and in which armies of sixty thousand men seldom came together, much less crossed the seas. Here was a whole fleet, numbering from a hundred to a hundred and fifty sail, nearly all great ships. It has eleven thousand

Resumé of the Spanish armament.

Showing its rare equipment.

veterans, nearly as many recruits, on board, some two thousand noble volunteers. It has over eight thousand sailors, and nearly half that number of guns. It has about three hundred barefooted friars and inquisitors, and a total tonnage of sixty thousand tons. Such a fleet had never before invaded any land. How can it fail, under such favouring circumstances, in such a holy cause, with so many prayers, said superstitious Catholics? Surely, said they, when to this great, this invincible Armada is conjoined the veteran army of Parma—some sixty thousand strong—all moving under the command of the greatest general of the age, England must speedily fall, and glory cover Spain and all her invading force! The King who rules in heaven had otherwise determined.

An unequalled force of invasion.

How, said many, can it fail?

CHAPTER VIII.

VARIOUS DELAYS IN THE SAILING OF THE ARMADA.

MANY unforeseen occurrences conspired to retard preparations for and delay the time of the Armada's sailing. When (in 1585) the king reached a settled purpose—or as settled as he was capable of reaching—to invade England, he thought his plans could be carried into effect the following year. It was, however, soon ascertained that neither a sufficiently strong fleet nor properly equipped army could be put in readiness for that year. There seemed little doubt, however, that if resources, energy and skill could succeed, all would be in readiness in 1587. In the

The king's plan of at once invading England impossible.

It cannot be done in 1586.

Again, in 1587.

spring of that year squadrons of ships were beginning to float in every considerable harbour of Spain and Portugal from Biscay to Cadiz. Many were hastening to the common rendezvous in Lisbon. An unexpected and somewhat alarming interruption again occurred, and caused a still further delay.

An unexpected disaster causes further delay.

On the second of April, Admiral Drake, who had already done much damage to Spanish shipping and commerce in the West Indies and on the ocean, appeared with a squadron of twenty-six English ships off the harbour of Cadiz, on the south of the peninsula. He found much shipping in the harbour, a squadron about to sail for Lisbon, and great naval stores ready for transportation and use. He had come out from Plymouth on this expedition to ascertain what reality there was in the rumours of preparation for the invasion of England, and, if opportunity presented itself, to strike an early blow. He wrote to Walshingham, in his own peculiar style, on the morning of his departure from Plymouth. Said he: "The wind commands me away. Our ships are under sail. God grant we may so live in His fear as the

Admiral Drake makes a descent on Cadiz and destroys many valuable stores and ships.

Drake's letter on the day he starts on his expedition.

enemy shall have cause to say that God doth fight for her majesty as well abroad as at home."*

Drake enters Cadiz on the 9th of April. On the ninth of the same month he dashed into the harbour of Cadiz in the face of the

---

* Admiral Drake, the hero o the struggle with the Armada, was the son of a Kentish clergyman of the Puritan stamp, to which party in the Church Drake inclined, if he did not actually belong. He possessed many high virtues beside capacity, talent, enterprise and experience. He was renowned for moral courage, integrity, trust in God, devotion to duty and to his country. He reminds us in many respects of the Protector, Oliver Cromwell, who appears in English history more than half a century later; notably in his religious phraseology, his boldness of action, his conviction that God was on his side, that he could not fail in his battles because the Divine arm, on which he trusted, never failed. Of all this his words, actions and sentiments, recorded in this little volume, give ample evidence. Here is a specimen: He says:— "Powerful as the Spaniards were, they were still but sons of mortal men, for the most part enemies to the truth, upholders of Dagon's image, which had already fallen before the Ark; so long as their ships would float, and they had food to eat, he and his men were ready to stay on the coast, and he was especially anxious the queen should allow him to do so; the continuing to the end yielded the true glory; if Hannibal had followed his victories he would never have been taken by Scipio; and when men thoroughly believed that what they were doing was in defence of their religion and country, a merciful God for Christ's sake would give them victory, nor would Satan and his ministers prevail against them."

great guns frowning from the fortress upon him, in spite of six large galeases at the entrance of the harbour, into the very midst of a large squadron ready to sail for the general rendezvous at Lisbon. He made himself master of the harbour, destroyed or captured, between galleons and store ships, over one hundred, and over ten thousand tons of lading, —raisins, dried fruits, biscuits, etc., all in less than thirty-six hours. Then on his return, off the coast of Portugal, and at Cape St. Vincent, he destroyed or captured more than three score vessels of all sizes. He also threatened Lisbon, and challenged the Spanish admiral, Santa Cruz, to come out with his ships and fight him in the open sea. The admiral declined the contest, and allowed him without molestation to complete his work of destruction. He was about to engage in the daring enterprise of investing the city of Lisbon, when he received orders from the queen, who was prosecuting peace negotiations with Parma, to return to England. He abandoned his enterprise and set sail the next morning for England. Thus, in his own quaint words, "he singed the king's beard." And besides getting certain knowledge

Marginal notes:
- Destroys one hundred vessels, ten thousand tons valuable provisions.
- Raids Cape St. Vincent.
- Challenges the Spanish admiral at Lisbon to fight him.
- He "singed the king's beard."

of the preparations that were being made, he learned a useful lesson as to the best modes of handling the light and active English ships against the large and heavy galleons of Spain. This bold and successful raid so affected the preparations of the Armada that all could not be got in readiness before the opening of the next year. This gave England further time for preparation.

He delayed their readiness for a year.

To the Marquis of Santa Crux, who had been in charge of all the preparations of the fleet, the king committed its supreme command, with the title and dignity of Captain-General of the Armada. When, however, all was ready for sailing, this brave officer, worn with the cares of the preparation, and chilled by the coldness towards him of his master, fell ill of a violent fever, and suddenly died.

Learned how to handle the Spanish ships.

Admiral Sauta Crux dies as the Armada is ready is sail.

In his stead the king appointed the Duke of Medina Sidonia—a man of noble family and plentiful fortune, but with very little knowledge or experience of service upon the sea. It was pertinently remarked at the time that "the king had succeeded the iron marquis with a golden duke." The vice-admiral also died about the same time, and in as unex-

The Duke of Medina Sidonia appointed Captain-general in his stead.

pected a manner; his successor has been already named. These changes, unfortunate for Spain, proved advantageous to England. They delayed the sailing of the fleet for a month, and so gave the English a little longer time to prepare. They also offered them less experience with which to contend when the great struggle came.

The Armada sails on the 28th of May, 1588.

At length, on the twenty-eighth of May, 1588, Admiral Medina Sidonia issued the orders to be observed on this voyage to the shores of England. On the next day, a signal-gun being fired, the whole Armada, consisting of ten squadrons, dropped down the Tagus from under the towers of Belim, led by the squadron of the captain-general. As he left the harbour he sounded his trumpet, every captain instantly did the same, and the whole Armada put to sea with a grand blare of trumpets. Thus, in a most imposing style, the fleet swept out to sea, entered the vast Atlantic, and turned their prows northward toward the shores of England. All hearts were full of confidence and hope, anticipating a prosperous voyage, a happy meeting with the troops of Parma, and a speedy conquest of England.

Leaves the Tagus and enters the sea with grand roll of trumpets.

ENGLAND'S VICTORY OVER THE ARMADA.

The Armada designated and esteemed by common consent Invincible.

All regarded the proud fleet as *Invincible*, and so gave it the designation, which has ever since, with an unrelenting irony, clung to it.

A storm falls on the Armada off the coast of Spain and disables it.

Before they had reached Cape Finisterre, the most northerly point of Spain, a violent storm overtook them, which seriously broke and scattered the fleet. Some ships were lost, many disabled, and all the remainder were in need of repair.

Puts into Corunna.

They therefore put into Corunna to refit. For a whole month the fleet lay in the harbour having everything again put in readiness for sea, and waiting for favourable weather.

Elizabeth, hearing of the disaster, advises Admiral Howard to lay up his ships and dismiss a part of his sailors.

Exaggerated news of this disaster soon reached England. Queen Elizabeth, thinking the invasion would not be again attempted that season, and eager to economize, advised Admiral Howard to lay up his ships in Plymouth and dismiss a portion of his sailors.

Admiral Howard reconnoitres the Armada.

Before acting on this economical advice the admiral thought it most patriotic first to ascertain how much harm had been wrought by the storm. He also hoped that, perchance, he might co-operate with the elements in further crippling the Armada. Accordingly he sallied out from Plymouth with a portion of his fleet,

Finds it not seriously damaged. steering toward Corunna. But learning the fleet had not been so badly disabled as reported, and seeing the winds favourable for bearing them toward England, he feared they might reach it in his absence, and so he speedily retraced his course to Plymouth. He had not yet begun to dispose of his ships or *Urges renewed preparations.* diminish his staff of sailors, but, on the contrary, urged more earnestly increased preparation for the approach of the invincible Armada, which he knew would soon appear.

Parma, in a spirit of dissimulation, negotiates for peace. During the delay caused in the sailing of the Armada, the Duke of Parma, by the directions of Philip, amused and engaged Elizabeth in meaningless peace negotiations. The queen sent plenipotentiaries to treat of the business in Flanders. The Hollanders utterly refused to participate in the negotiations. England and Spain carried them on for some time, especially dealing with preliminaries. Spain dissembled and concealed her designs, for she was at the same time increasing her preparations *The queen also desired it if possible.* for the invasion. The queen wished peace, but a peace without sacrificing the Netherlands, was impossible. That Elizabeth would have yielded to such treachery toward her Protestant allies is hardly credible. She, too, may have been gaining time to prepare for a struggle, which she still hoped might be averted. Elizabeth looked with comparative indifference on the religious aspects of the struggle of the Netherlands. But the growing fanaticism of the Catholics, the prevailing importunities of the Jesuits—Allen and Parsons and Co.—with Philip, and the various atrocities which had been committed by the Spanish and French Catholics, aroused the Protestants of England, whose zeal more than compensated for the queen's apathy. The tidings which, from time to time, reached the people through returned soldiers, officers, refugees or travellers (newspapers were as yet hardly known),* of

<small>The zeal of the English.</small>

<small>Stimulated to the highest pitch by the atrocities committed against the Protestants of France and the Netherlands.</small>

---

* It is of interest to notice the entrance into life, in the midst of the excitements and solicitudes of 1588, of that new and powerful agent for speedily spreading among the people intelligence of matters of public interest—THE NEWSPAPER. Till this time despatches and brief notices from the Government to the people were made in writing. Matters of more detail, on politics, or observance of the laws, were circulated in pamphlets. The convenience of combining in one these two modes of communicating with the people became apparent to the Ministry. Accordingly, in April, 1588, the first number of the *English Mercury* was issued for this purpose, and seems thereafter to have appeared daily, or almost every day. There is framed, in the British Museum, a copy of this paper, dated July

Alva's butcheries in the Low Countries—the horrid massacre of St. Bartholomew, the assassination of William the Silent of Orange, the like attempts on the queen herself, the intolerant spirit of Spain and the cruelties of the Spanish Inquisition—these revived in the people memories of the tragic scenes of Queen Mary's day, and stimulated the spirit of Protestantism to the highest pitch. The people's spirit and purpose of resistance to Catholicism was far stronger than the queen's. The English people were thoroughly imbued with the love of liberty and independence, and they were determined to contend for the right to enjoy them.

The people in advance of the queen.

Queen Elizabeth's hopes of success with Philip did not spring from a belief she could outrival him in military force and appliances, but from her knowledge of his character. His temper was slow, hesitating, and over-cautious. He was always waiting and watching for a greater advantage. Elizabeth was active, versatile, abrupt but bold in her movements, and acted promptly when she saw an advantage.

Elizabeth's hope of success lay in Philip's hesitating temper.

23rd, which is marked Number Fifty, pointing back to the date of its first publication.

CHAPTER IX.

ENGLAND'S DANGER.

Was England prepared?

HAVING briefly described the causes and design, pointed out the plans, preparations and movements of the force of invasion, let us now inquire what was the state of things in England, and what preparations were there being made to resist the attack of so formidable a power.

The peril of England great. She is self-reliant and confident.

There is no use in trying to conceal the greatness or manifoldness of the peril in which England at that moment stood. From a purely human point of view, it seems to us she had far more ground for fear than hope, for dismay than confidence; yet brave, self-reliant and patriotic, she did not for a moment quail or waver. But she resolutely set herself to the work laid on her, determined to do her whole duty and confide the results to the Supreme Disposer of all things.

In the first place, she was in danger from the devotees of the papacy who were in England. That system had then many adherents in the country. Fully one-half the population still adhered to the Catholic Church. Every consideration calculated to arouse their religious zeal and sectarian bitterness was spread in glaring colours before them. Pope Sixtus the Fifth, noted no less for his capacity than for his intolerance, heartily espoused the enterprise. He had been the animating spirit of the abortive plot for the murder of Queen Elizabeth, and the advancement of Mary Queen of Scots to the English throne. He longed to see the power of Protestantism broken by whatever means. As England was its stronghold, she must first be crushed, if it is to fall. He gives up his temporary enmity to Philip, and they become friends, as long before Pilate had done with Herod, that they may destroy One who had done them no wrong. For he is determined to re-establish the religion of Rome in England, although its queen and people are opposed. For this object he directed his spiritual thunders against the queen. Though she did not belong to his communion, he enforced the bull of excommunication his predecessor had issued against her. He branded her name with infamy. He deposed her from her throne and deprived her of her kingdom, though his supremacy was not acknowledged in England. He absolved her subjects from obedience and oaths of allegiance to her, and proclaimed a crusade against England, as a nation of heretics and infidels. He also granted plenary indulgence to all who would participate in the crusade and engage in the invasion. This warlike pontiff did yet more. To stimulate Philip's zeal and strengthen his hands in this work of religion, he entered into a treaty with him, promising him an immense subsidy the moment the first English port came into the possession of Spain. He encouraged his adherents in England and his followers elsewhere with the promise of rewards, if they promptly and liberally co-operated in the enterprise. He felt confident of a grand and immediate success.

Deprives the queen of her kingdom, and absolves her subjects from obligation to her.

He also promises material aid.

Invites the co-operation of the faithful.

The plot for the assassination of Queen Elizabeth.

It may be well, in passing, to present to our readers the leading historical facts concerning the plot (in 1586) for the assassination of Queen Elizabeth, in which both the pope and the

King of Spain were implicated. The conception of it sprung out of the pope's bull excomunicating the queen, and from the zeal of the "Most Catholic King" for the enforcement of that decree. The principal agent, however, in organizing the plot, was John Ballard, a Jesuit and Seminary priest, who considered himself called to give effect to that part of the pope's bull, which authorizes the removal of the excommunicate from among the living.

The Jesuit, John Ballard, the principal agent in the plot.

Ballard had obtained the pope's sanction to the plot, and secretly pressed forward his scheme to accomplishment. Disguised in dress and name, Ballard travelled over England as Captain Fortescue, conferring with young Catholics, and inciting them to engage in his enterprise. This included a Catholic insurrection in England as well as the assassination of the queen. The plan was for the Catholics to rise in mass as soon as the queen had been dispatched, liberate the Queen of Scots from her imprisonment, proclaim her Queen of England, and thus through her, draw off England and reunite her to Rome. Many Catholic noblemen espoused the cause: lords

The Pope's sanction given. Philip of Spain to co-operate.

Seize the Queen of Scots, liberate her, and proclaim her Queen of England.

Thus would England be again united under her to the

ENGLAND'S VICTORY OVER THE ARMADA. 67

Church of Rome.

Percy Arundel, Henry Howard, Stanley, and others, had bound themselves by an oath to stand by one another and the Church of Rome. Others were ready to co-operate with the Scotch Catholic lords—Maxwell, Huntley, and Claude Hamilton—in effecting a revolt, and so uniting Scotland and England in Mary's crown.

Babington, of Derbyshire, the chief actor in carrying out the plot of assassination.

The man most active in executing the details of the plot of assassination in England was Anthony Babington, of Derbyshire, a susceptible young gentleman of some fortune and culture, who had come under the spell of Mary's fascinations and had devoted himself to her cause.

Six young men of the queen's household enter the plot.

Babington had access to Queen Elizabeth's household, to which many Catholics freely resorted, and taking dishonourable advantage of his privilege, he enticed six young men, who belonged to the queen's household and had constant access to her person, to promise to kill her, stabbing her, or in some safe way dispatching her; the condition of their so doing being the co-operation of the insurgent Catholics, and of the King of Spain, to liberate the Queen of Scots and place her on the English throne.

Ballard informs Philip of the ripeness of his scheme and seeks assurance of his help.

Ballard went back to the continent, assured Philip all was arranged; that the English Catholic nobles were ready to move, had even bound themselves by an oath to rise as one man when the King of Spain assured them of his readiness to co-operate with his forces in placing the new queen upon the throne.

Walshingham discovers the plot and brings the guilty to the gallows.

Walshingham had discovered the plot, secured copies of the correspondence of Babington, Ballard and others in the plot. In fact, he knew more about it, in a short time, than any one of the conspirators. When the proper moment came and the scheme was ripe, the conspirators were arrested: they were put on trial. The proof was full and undeniable. The guilty received the legal rewards of their treasonable conduct. Terror, exasperation and dread of coming evils agitated the hearts of all Catholics.

Dangers apprehended from Scotland.

But besides her danger from her Catholic people, she was also in danger from her neighbour on the north. James VI. of Scotland was the son of Mary, Queen of Scots, who had, a few months before, been executed in England for treason.

James VI. approached by Philip, but secured in the Eng-

Through his agents, well supplied with Spanish gold, it was known Philip was making every effort to induce James to join the Spanish cause. Thus it was suggested to him he could, as in filial duty he was bound, execute righteous vengeance for the execution of his mother. James knew, however, how that mother had murdered his own father and had plotted to deprive him of his royal birthright in Scotland. Besides, it was known that lords Huntley, Maxwell and other Catholics had formed plans for organizing and putting in motion a revolutionary force as the basis of a Spanish movement in Scotland; or at least for a diversion of the English army so as to weaken its strength against the army of invasion which it would have to meet in England.

Queen Elizabeth sends commissioners to James; he also writes him.

To meet and overcome these dangers, Queen Elizabeth sent commissioners to Scotland to treat with James and secure him in the interests of England and of Protestantism, which he professed to believe. She also wrote to him in her own hand, presenting, as it is said, "stout arguments," liberal promises and large payments.

The Church of Scotland also addresses him.

The Church of Scotland, which was much interested in their young king's adhesion to England, exerted their influence with him both on the ground of his own prospective interests as heir of the English crown, and on the ground of his profession of the reformed religion.* James was secured, and with him Scotland.

The three powerful feelings or impulses which ruled Philip.

We may observe three powerful feelings or impulses in Philip, by one or the other of which all his public actions were influenced. These were ambition, religion and revenge. The Protestants had successfully resisted his persecuting measures in the Netherlands. He had been thwarted in all his schemes for bringing them to submit to the authority of the papal church, and respect the persecuting edicts of the king and "the Holy Office" of the Inquisition. This, he believed, was mainly due to the intervention of English power and influence. He also had titular claims on the sovereignty of England. He had, as husband of his cousin, the late Queen Mary, eldest daughter of Henry VIII., been styled King of England. After Mary's death the insolent islanders had indeed refused to longer recognize the title. He had, however, never ceased to regard it, and longed for an opportunity of making it good. His ambition would, perhaps, have been already gratified, had not the Princess Elizabeth stood

Philip's schemes of ambition thwarted by England.

Will enforce his title in England as he had done in Portugal

---

* Hetherington, Hist. of Ch. of Scotland, *in loco.*

in the way. Then England would have been an appanage of Spain. But had he not successfully asserted a like claim in right of his deceased wife, Maria of Portugal, only a few years before? Had he not conquered that country and made it part of his dominions?

reach of Philip's ambition.

Why not now do the same in England? He determines, therefore, to secure it by the force of arms and the arbitrament of war. When that is done his Netherland subjects, he thinks, will yield to his will, and even France, which he now divides into two camps—Catholic and Huguenot—will soon fall exhausted under the strain of the conflict. So far does his ambition reach.

ks revenge for ly ilts.

He had also, he thought, great wrongs to avenge. In this lay the deepest motive of his great undertaking. He had, as sovereign of the greatest nation of Europe, been insulted by England. In the first place, she had refused to acknowledge him as her king. Besides, her present queen had rejected his earnest suit, after encouraging it. She had, moreover, in disregard of his intervention, given the head of the Catholic Queen of Scots to the block. The flag of Spain had been insulted on the high seas: many of his ships, with much treasure, had been made prizes by Drake, Hawkins, and other English sailors. England's queen had looked on approvingly, instead of punishing the leaders in these foul deeds. England must now drink to the dregs the cup of retribution which he had poured out for her. The invincible Armada will begin, Parma's army and the Inquisition will complete her subjugation and conversion.

CHAPTER X.

ENGLAND'S DANGER ON THE PAPAL SIDE.

PHILIP claimed, however, that his supreme motive in this great "enterprise," as he called it, was the love of God and the honour of religion. By which he meant the coercion into submission to the Church of Rome of all dissentients. In this work he claimed to be the leader and champion. "The point," says Hume, "on which Philip rested his highest glory, the perpetual object of his policy, was to support orthodoxy, and exterminate heresy." He zealously employed that bloody machine, the Spanish Inquisition, which, with its swarms of monks and familiars, as spies, and Dominicans and Jesuits, as executioners, had already immolated thousands of unoffending Moslems, Jews, and Protestants, in the Spanish kingdom. In the name of religion, and for the glory of God, he proposed introducing it into England, so soon as the Armada had effected the safe landing of his soldiers, and the conquest of the Island was made sure. Thus he would convert England, and restore her people to the arms of their loving mother, the Church of Rome.

England to be converted by force of arms and the Inquisition.

Philip was, in truth, a cruel and fanatical bigot—the impersonation of all that is narrow, obstinate and hateful in religion. He was sullen and ungenial in his temper, hard and implacable in his resentments, and inhuman in the cruelties he wantonly inflicted on thousands of his fellow-creatures. He could witness the tortures and hear the cries of anguish of an *auto-da-fé*, as he often did, and, without a spark of feeling for the innocent sufferers, cry, "So let all Thy enemies perish, O Lord." He was far happier when executing the most savage vengeance than in exercising the most becoming clemency. Let me here present a picture of his bearing and part in one of these blood-freezing scenes—the celebration of an *auto-da-fé* in the fair Spanish city of Valladolid, in 1559. Early in that year, Philip finding that, notwithstanding all his vigilance, the Lutheran doctrines were spreading, wrote to

Philip a fanatical bigot.

A cold-blooded persecutor.

the pope for further power, if that might be given, to increase the stringency of the "Holy Office of the Inquisition." His Holiness, approving the fidelity of the king, issued a bull, directing the Inquisitor-General Valdez to consign to the flames all imprisoned as suspects, relapsed persons, or known heretics. This gentle order Valdez cheerfully proceeded to execute.

The pope's bull to the Inquisitor-Gen. Valdez to burn the prisoners.

In the autumn of 1559, after the king's return to Spain from the Low Countries, in conformity to the pope's bull Valdez celebrated one of a series of *autos-da-fé*,* which had been in progress during the summer, both that he might honor the king and publicly exhibit his zeal on behalf of religion.

He proceeds to do so by celebrating a series of autos-da-fé, one in Valladolid, in which the king took part.

On October 8th, a company of victims —who had been detained, some of them a

---

* An auto-da-fé, or *act of faith*, was a public solemnity observed by the Court of the Inquisition, at which those who had fallen under sentence of the Court had their sentence and punishment publicly announced. The victims were then delivered over to the secular power, which inflicted forthwith the death penalty upon them. The execution of the victims, with whatever form and variety of torture the Court had recommended, was publicly and promptly proceeded with, in presence of the Inquisitors, Princes, Grandees, and Ecclesiastics, and all who chose to be present.

long time, in the dungeons of the Inquisition, and among whom were persons of rank and learning—were brought out before an august assemblage in the city of Valladolid, for celebrating an *auto-da-fé*.

Takes a conspicuous part.

The king was seated on a throne on an elevated platform, beside him his sister and his son. All the civil and ecclesiastical dignitaries of the land—many nobles, foreign ministers and clergy, and a great concourse of people were present.

The sermon by the Bishop of Cunca.

The sermon (for such gentle address always preceded this Christian entertainment) was preached by the Bishop of Cunca. The inquisitor-general then arose, and said aloud: "O God, make speed to help us!" The king drew his sword, and Valdez, approaching him,

The king's oath administered by the Inquisitor-General Valdez.

read the king's oath: "Your Majesty swears by the cross of the sword, whereon your royal hand reposes, that you will give all necessary favour to the Holy Office of the Inquisition against heretics, apostates, and those who favour them, and will denounce and inform against all those who, to your royal knowledge, shall act or speak against the faith."

The king answered in an audible voice, "I swear it!" and signed the paper.

Immediately the fires were kindled and thirteen distinguished victims were burned alive before the king's eyes.

<small>Thirteen victims burned.</small>

Also the body of a victim whom a timeous death had snatched from the hands of the Holy Office.

Among them was a young nobleman of high character and commanding talents, named Carlos de Sessa. As the king passed from the platform to the stake, De Sessa said to him, "How can you look on and permit me to be burned?" The king made the cruel but characteristic reply, "I would carry the wood to burn my own son withal, were he as wicked as you."*

<small>DeSessa's request. The king's heartless reply.</small>

---

* Dr. McCree, in his History of the Reformation in Spain, describes a general *auto-da-fé* as follows:—"In it a number of heretics were brought out, and the celebration was performed with imposing solemnity, and formed an imitation of a Roman triumph, combined with that of the last Judgment. It was always celebrated on a Sunday or holiday, in the largest church, but more frequently on the most spacious square of the town in which it happened to be held. Intimation of this was publicly made beforehand, in all the churches and religious houses of the neighbourhood. The attendance of the civil authorities, as well as the clergy, secular and regular, was required; and with the view of attracting the multitude, an indulgence of forty days was proclaimed to all who should witness the ceremonies."

Philip had not only been privy to, but an accomplice in, the terrible massacre of St. Bartholomew, which cut off at one fell stroke not much less than a hundred thousand Huguenots. His expressions of joy and approval of the cowardly conduct of the King of France, in that cruel scene, are revolting and heartless. Says the French envoy then at the court of Spain: "The king, on receiving the intelligence, was more delighted than with all the good fortune of his life, declared that Charles IX., and no one else, deserved the title 'Most Christian King.'" He sent his felicitations to the envoy, and added: "I am just going to St. Jerome's to render thanks to God, and to offer prayer for his Majesty of France that he may receive divine support in so great an affair."

He approved of the Bartholomew's massacre.

Praised Charles IX. of France for the horrid butchery

About the same date Philip wrote to the Duke of Alva, in the Netherlands, in regard to certain French prisoners, to the number of one thousand, who had been taken by Alva on the field. Many of them were persons of distinction, who, at that date, lay in the gaols and prisons of the Netherlands. Philip issued this horrible order of wholesale murder: "I desire, if you have not already disembarrassed the

The cruel contribution of one thousand French Protestants made by Philip to the horrid tragedy of St. Bartholomew in the Netherlands.

world of them, you will do it immediately, and inform me thereof, for I see no reason why it should be deferred."

In this cold-blooded and inhuman manner he sent a thousand French Protestants, all of them prisoners of war, to instant execution. This was his contribution to the sum total of the horrors of the tragedy of St. Bartholomew.

<small>Assassination included in the system of government of the King of Spain.</small>
Philip regarded assassination as an important and proper part of his system of government. He had successfully employed it to remove persons who stood in the way of his schemes. He had a bureau of assassination, which was situated at Brussels, as the point most convenient to the victims he wished to dispatch. The Count of Fuentes—an intriguing and unscrupulous, but persistent and plausible minion—was appointed its head.

<small>The rewards he offered for the assassination of the Prince William of Orange.</small>
The liberal rewards he offered for the assassination of William the Silent, induced several miscreants, at different times, to attempt the life of this, the most virtuous, wise and patriotic citizen of Holland. At length, on the 10th of July, 1584, he was cut off by one of them —Balthaser Gerard. Philip, on receiving certain information that the deed was done,

coldly remarked: "If it had only been two years earlier, much trouble might have been spared me; but it is better late than never." In recognition of these disreputable services the blood-guilty king ennobled the family of Gerard, and endowed it with an estate taken from the children of the man he had murdered.

The cold-blooded remark of Philip on being informed of the assassination of the Prince of Orange.

He also wished, as did his holiness the pope, a like end for the Protestant princes—Henry of Navarre and Elizabeth of England. The proof of these matters is now abundant. We shall wait to cite only a single case in evidence—that of the English envoy at the court of France in 1584, at the very time William of Orange had been assassinated. The envoy wrote home immediately after the occurrence of that tragic event. Said he: "From information gathered at the Spanish minister's house, there were more than two or three about to execute the same practice upon her majesty, and that within two months. Therefore exercise the greatest vigilance, and eschew the danger."

He wished to see the same end brought to Henry of Navarre and Queen Elizabeth.

Both Philip and the pope confidently looked to their English co-religionists for co-operation and help against the queen. The Jesuits and

Philip and the pope expected the co-operation

seminary priests had already tried their skill in many dark and treasonable plots for dispatching her, and raising to the English throne her faithless rival the Queen of Scots. Many of these emissaries had been banished, but some still skulked among their Romish confederates. There were many undoubtedly among the English Catholics, who in heart favoured the Spanish project, and who desired reunion with the Church of Rome. But they regarded organization or open expressions of sympathy alike impolitic and dangerous. In general, they were unwilling to exchange their English independence for Spanish subjection and submission; though they would willingly have exchanged the Established Church of England at any moment for the Church of Rome. It is true the queen and government found stringent measures necessary to prevent conspiracies and repress outbreaks in this element of the population; but it is also true that while such measures were enacted, it was not often found necessary to put them in practice. They were enforced only against such as allied themselves with traitors or enemies. Individually, Roman Catholics were treated with

[Marginalia: the English Catholics. The Catholics did not wish to lose their English independence, but preferred the Romish Church. Strict measures required to repress outbreaks. Stringent measures enacted, but enforced only when reason or time rendered it necessary.]

the same tolerance as Protestants. They were not excluded from the army or navy, nor from any part of the queen's service. In proof of this impartiality, the queen appointed Lord Howard of Effingham, a Roman Catholic peer, Lord Admiral of England and commander of all her fleet. There were also Roman Catholic landed proprietors, who, prompted by interest, or their convictions of duty, or perhaps by loyalty to their rightful sovereign, organized their tenants into military companies, and tendered their services to the queen. These gentlemen knew the baseness of the libels, and falseness of the slanders which the priests and Jesuits—such men as Allen, Campion and Ballard—had so assiduously spread about the queen. Instead of giving credence to, or feeling sympathy with them, they aroused indignation and disgust. We introduce the following note at the close of this chapter to show our readers the objects and designs of those English Catholics who had recently founded seminaries and colleges to train priests for England, in Spain, Flanders and Rome.

"In order to uphold their violent ultramontane policy *seminaries* were founded, in which young men were trained for missionary work in England, and led to believe that the conversion of their countrymen and the deposition of the heretical queen were objects worth any risk to accomplish. The principal intriguer, who was also the founder of the first English seminary at Douai, in Flanders (1568), was Wm Allen, once a fellow of Oriel College, Oxford, afterwards a cardinal. This man procured the establishment of English colleges both at Rome and in Spain, besides that at Douai. In 1580 he sent into England the first Jesuit missionaries, Fathers Parsons and Campion. These men were pledged to do the mandates of a church which had excommunicated and deposed the queen—came, in fact, as traitors to the government, and could expect nothing when apprehended but the treatment of traitors. At the time of the Armada, Parsons and Allen put forth a book openly advocating the cause of the King of Spain against Elizabeth. Plots against the life of the queen were continually being organized by some of these intriguers."*

---

* Dean Perry's History of the Church of England.

CHAPTER XI.

ENGLAND'S DANGER, FROM A MILITARY POINT OF VIEW.

England's condition on military grounds not encouraging.

ENGLAND'S condition was insecure and her coasts much exposed in a military point of view. She had no standing army except the queen's guards and a few garrison troops on the northern border. The queen's revenues were unequal to maintain a larger force. She had no allies on the continent, except the Protestants of the Netherlands. She was not sure whether the King of Scots would continue true to her cause. And she had reason to fear the sympathies of her Catholic subjects might carry them over to the

The hope of the cause and of the war lay in the liberality and patriotism of the people.

side of Spain. The safety of the country at that crisis really fell into the hands and on the shoulders of the liberal and loyal people of England themselves. If they did not respond on a scale adequate to the emergency—if they did not furnish the means and men for the war—all would be lost. The temper and patriotism of the nation, however, was then higher than that of the queen, and quite equal to that of her foremost statesmen and sea-captains.

Her resources and population were then comparatively small. She was ill prepared for carrying on either offensive or defensive war; and she had hitherto made very little preparation for meeting her invaders. Both on her coast and in the interior her defences were few and feeble. Her power of resisting an attack from the sea on any part of her coast consisted of a few crumbling towers scattered at great distances along her seaboard, not one of which was capable of resisting a formidable attack. "They were better calculated," it has been justly said, "to repel a few bands of sea robbers, than the great force of the Spanish invasion." The strong feudal castles, which in earlier times protected the interior and gave a sense of security to the people, had either fallen into decay or been converted into baronial residences, and were utterly incapable of sustaining an attack of the artillery of the time. The whole coast from Cornwall to Kent, from the

Lizard to the North Foreland, was without any adequate fortification. There was no place of strength into which the queen, in case of an emergency, could escape with confidence of finding even temporary security.

No adequate coast protection.

No danger was more likely to prove fatal to England's cause at the last moment than the queen's own reluctance, her persistent refusal, to believe that the great preparations of Spain were to be directed against her kingdom—with such consummate duplicity and crafty dissimulation did the Duke of Parma carry on peace negotiations with her up to the summer of 1588.

England's danger from the queen's disbelief of Philip's design of invading England.

Her great and true minister, Walshingham, who well knew the designs of Parma's preparations, and the drift of his actions, even to his purchase of trappings and finery to be worn by his victorious soldiers on entering London, could not induce her to believe that she was in danger.

Would not believe Walshingham, who knew.

So carefully had Parma kept his secret, and so skilfully had he executed his part of the king's plot, that few of Philip's ministers or court knew when the fleet would sail, or to what point it might move. During the winter preceding the invasion Philip wrote to his chief, the Duke of Parma, in the Low Countries, thus charging

Deceived her with peace negotiations till the last.

Philip to Parma.

him :—"Keep secret the plot of the invasion, protract your peace negotiations, shift the points in discussion to save time, conclude nothing, and so blind the eyes of the English as to the design of our preparations."

The English people more eager than the queen.

The boldest of England's sea-captains, such as Drake, Hawkins, and Frobisher, felt chagrined and disappointed that they were neither allowed to strike disabling blows at the preparations of Spain, nor to press forward their own. They had seen service, encountered many dangers, and captured numerous prizes on distant seas. All these gallant men longed for action. Said Hawkins, "Let us have open war with the Jesuits. Then every man will contribute, fight, devise and do for the liberty of our country."

Hatred of the Jesuits

He hated, he said, the sneaky, underhand ways of the crafty and silent Jesuit. They were the emissaries of Philip and the Pope. He knew they had the spirit of their masters, and were always actuated by love of Rome and hatred of England, love of Popery and hatred of Protestantism.

Howard also preferred action to negotiation.

Admiral Howard, from his little flag-ship, the "Ark Royal," defiantly said, as tidings reach England magnifying the vastness of the Armada's preparations, "Let me have the four great ships and twenty hoys, with but twenty men apiece, and each with but two iron pieces, and her Majesty shall have a good account of the Spanish forces, and I will make the King of Spain wish his galleys home again."

<small>Only four large ships in the queen's navy.</small>

These four great ships were the principal ones in the queen's navy. They lay at their docks in Chatham. Howard wished them at once put in order and in action. For this he made fruitless entreaty to the queen. Her ear was still lulled and her heart inclined to rest in the plausible but dissembling negotiations of Parma, promising peace when he had no thoughts of peace.

In this place it may be proper to make a few observations in reference to the navy of Queen Elizabeth's day. It may strike us as

<small>No regularly organized naval department in the days of Elizabeth.</small>

strange, but it is nevertheless true, that England at that time had no such institution as a distinctly organized naval department, nor had she any staff of professional seamen in the service of the government. Whenever a

<small>Sea-captains and sailors taken from merchant ships, etc.</small>

necessity arose, the government solicited from among the sea-captains of the commercial marine such as had risen into notice by their

ENGLAND'S VICTORY OVER THE ARMADA. 89

own daring and success. Such were Drake, Hawkins and Frobisher. Nor had she any sailors in her service, but hired for a given period—a month, two or three months at a time—such as could do sailors' work, wherever they could be found.

The ships of small tonnage in that day. The largest merchant ships then in England did not exceed four hundred tons, and of them she had very few. Those armed cruisers, which had done such famous exploits and made such marvellous voyages, were no larger than the schooners of our time. The "Golden Hind," *The "Golden Hind" only one hundred tons.* in which Drake "ploughed his memorable furrow round the globe," was only one hundred tons burden.

The queen's navy consists of only thirty-four ships. The entire English navy had, all told, only thirty-four ships. Of these only thirteen were over four hundred tons, and sixteen were cutters, pinnaces or schooners, under that tonnage. *Only five large.* There were only five ships called large, and of these the greatest was only one thousand tons.

A commission, consisting of Burleigh, Walshingham, Drake, Howard and Frobisher, had been appointed four or five years before the invasion, to ascertain the condition of her majesty's ships, stores and supplies. This com-

7

mission recommended the construction of five larger ships, of new design, being longer of lines and not so wide as before. These were constructed as follows: The "Ark Royal" and the "Victory," eight hundred tons each; the "Bear" and the "Elizabeth Jonas," each nine hundred tons, and the "Triumph," of one thousand tons. These were the great ships of the queen's navy in 1588.

These five had been constructed not long before the war on the recommendation of a commission.

Lord Howard felt a keen disappointment at the queen's persistent refusal to allow even one of these great ships to take its place in the fleet. Said he, "When should she serve if not at such a time as this? Either she is fit now to serve, or is fit for the fire. I hope never to see in my time so great cause for her to be used. I dare say her majesty will look that men fight for her, and I know they will at this time. The King of Spain does not keep any ship at home, either of his own or any other that he can get for money."

Lord Howard's disappointment at the queen's refusal to let him use even one of her ships.

After all, it must be said, to the honour of queen and people, that when, at length, they became undeceived, and doubt gave way to the terrible certainty that the King of Spain was about to hurl the whole power of his king-

;edom on England for its conquest and overthrow, they did not quail or tremble, but with brave and courageous hearts, even with a sense of relief, set themselves with renewed purpose and energy to organize means of defence.

Mr. Motley eloquently describes the feeling of queen and people at that moment, as follows :—

"When the great queen, arousing herself from the delusion into which the falsehoods of France and of Philip had lulled her, should once more represent—as no man or woman better than Elizabeth Tudor could represent— the defiance of England to foreign insolence ; the resolve of a whole people to die rather than yield, there was a thrill of joy through the national heart. When the enforced restraint was at length taken off, there was one bound toward the enemy. Few more magnificent spectacles have been seen in history than the enthusiasm which pervaded the country as the great danger so long deferred was felt at last to be closely approaching. The little nation of four millions, the merry England of the sixteenth century, went forward to the death-grapple with its gigantic antagonist as cheerfully as to a long expected holiday. Spain was a vast empire, overshadowing the world; England, in comparison, but a province; yet nothing could surpass the steadiness with which the conflict was awaited."*

---

* Motley's U. N., p. 574.

CHAPTER XII.

ENGLAND'S PREPARATIONS FOR WAR—NAVAL AND MILITARY.

England's in hope her navy.

ENGLAND'S hope of defence lay largely in the brave and bold, if numerically inadequate, body of sailors she was able to muster; her regular soldiers, still fewer in number, and lacking in discipline, were loyal and patriotic. The queen's standing army in 1588 was, perhaps, little more than half the fourteen thousand which constitute, in 1888, the metropolitan police force of the great city of London. But her people were resolute and almost a unit in purpose to resist the invader *termines* to the last extremity. Walshingham, Raleigh *increase strength.* and other patriotic leaders, seeing the weakness of the coast defences, and knowing the hopelessness of soon strengthening them, concluded that as England's greatest power was on sea, it was best to increase the power of the navy by adding new ships and of greater tonnage; Though the queen, who then, as always, both preached and practised economy, did her utmost to infuse new vigour into this arm of the service. But it was now too late to build more ships. Many noblemen, merchants and seaport towns, however, provided at their own expense squadrons of ships fully furnished and equipped for the service. The chronicler, Stowe, relates the following incident, which shows the spirit of liberality in which the commercial people of the land helped in this great emergency :—

Ships provided by seaport towns, and merchants and gentlemen.

"The lord mayor and aldermen of the city of London having asked the lords of the commission on supplies what they considered the city should raise?" the lords answered, "Five thousand men and fifteen ships." The city authorities craved two days in which to prepare their answer. In replying, they begged their lordships to accept in token of their love and loyalty to queen and country, ten thousand men and thirty ships, all amply provided."

Incident of the city of London's liberality.

It may be added that the city of London contributed even more than this liberal contingent to the national cause, when the day of trial came.

Liberal contributions.

Little squadrons were rapidly prepared in

almost every English port along the Channel—in Dartmouth, Deptford, Harwich, Portsmouth, and Plymouth. In the last named harbour the queen's ships were collected. They numbered, all told, at that port, just thirty-four sail. Lord Howard was in command. His flagship, the "Ark Royal," was eight hundred tons, mounted fifty-five guns, and was manned by four hundred and twenty-five sailors. Next in command was Sir Francis Drake, vice-admiral. His flagship was the "Revenge," of five hundred tons, manned by two hundred and fifty sailors, and carrying forty guns. Lord Henry Seymour also commanded a squadron. His flagship was the "Rainbow," of five hundred tons, two hundred and fifty sailors, and forty guns. His squadron, composed of both Dutch and English ships, was instructed to cruise along the French coasts, off Gravelines, Dunkirk, Newport and the mouth of the Scheldt. An immense swarm of Dutch crafts of all sizes—fly-boats, schooners, fish-boats, gun-boats, blocaded the entrance of these harbours and watched the outlets through their sands and shallows. Thus the Duke of Parma could not

[Margin notes: The "Ark Royal," the admiral's flag-ship. The "Revenge," the vice-admiral's. The "Rainbow," Admiral Seymour's flagship. A fleet of small crafts watch the entrance of all the Flemish harbours.]

possibly get out into the English Channel, without a struggle.

Hawkins was rear-admiral; his flag-ship, the "Victory," of eight hundred tons. She was manned with four hundred sailors, and carried forty guns. Frobisher commanded the "Triumph." the largest ship in the fleet, her tonnage being eleven hundred tons; she was manned with five hundred sailors, and carried forty-two guns.

The comparative size of the ships of Elizabeth and Victoria. The size of the vessels of the fleet, though the largest of that age, seem in our day ridiculously small. A collier's brig of the present time is as large as the greatest merchantman which sailed from London in the days of Queen Elizabeth. There lies oftentimes, around a single pier in Liverpool in these days, a far greater ship tonnage than that of the whole English fleet which conquered the invincible Armada in 1588. Yet it is worth remembering, that all England's present eminence, as carrier of the world, must be traced to that time as its starting-point and true beginning.

Lord Howard's whole Plymouth fleet consisted, as already stated, of thirty-four ships.

ENGLAND'S VICTORY OVER THE ARMADA. 97

Howard's Plymouth fleet, 12,000 tons; 6,279 soldiers; 837 guns.

Their aggregate tonnage was less than twelve thousand tons. Their seamen were six thousand two hundred and seventy-nine; and their armament eight hundred and thirty-seven guns. So rapidly, however, did private liberality increase the fleet that by mid-summer

The whole number of vessels, 150-190.

the number of sail had reached one hundred and fifty, perhaps nearly two hundred. Many of them were, however, mere coasters and traders of less than a hundred tons burden. Not ten perhaps, all told, were of more than five hundred tons, and only one reached a thousand tons.

Whole number of sailors 15-785.

The number of sailors of the whole fleet was fifteen thousand seven hundred and eighty-five, which included both seamen and fighting men. For in the English fleet they were one

The Spanish soldiers did not work the ships.

and the same. On the Spanish galleons, the mariners were not soldiers. Besides these, they had a large force of galley slaves. The soldiers were provided for and waited on in a style

The English wait on themselves, work the ships and fight.

quite unknown in the English service. Our tars had both to work the ship, wait on themselves, and do the fighting. They preferred their independent position, and yet rendered, as the world knows, no mean account of themselves when the day of conflict came. Thus the tonnage of our ships, the number of our men, and the might of our armament were not half as great as those of the Spanish fleet.

THE ENGLISH ARMY.

The regular army small.

It is reorganized in two grand divisions.

The regular army was then very small, consisting of not more than six or eight thousand men. The Earl of Leicester, Lord Lunsden, and Sir Francis Walshingham undertook its reorganization and enlargement, with the purpose of forming two large armies, one for the coast and the other for the interior. The army for the coast was to have twenty-seven thousand infantry, and two thousand cavalry, and to be stationed at Tilbury, near the mouth of the Thames. The other was to have several camps in the interior, and was to consist of at least thirty-six thousand foot, and such cavalry force as could be secured, and was designed for the protection of the queen. Its centre of opera-

The Earl of Leicester commander-in-chief.

His camp at Tilbury.

tion was London. Her Majesty appointed her favourite, the Earl of Leicester, commander-in-chief of her whole army, with his headquarters at Tilbury. She appointed her relative, Lord

ENGLAND'S VICTORY OVER THE ARMADA. 99

Lord Lunsden in command of the army of the interior.

Lunsden, to the army of the interior, with power to move his camp when necessary.

The camp of Tilbury.

The army of the Earl of Leicester was put under drill, and his camp became the centre of interest to the country as well as the army. Though he was to have twenty-seven thousand choice men, he never had in fact more than seventeen. It was composed chiefly of train-bands from the adjacent counties. Queen Elizabeth now threw herself heartily into the interests of the war. She soon became the life and soul of all the preparations and training of the camp at Tilbury. She passed freely among and reviewed the troops and inspected the new battalions. She encouraged discipline, which was sorely needed, smiled graciously on the men as she passed among them, and by her animated and cheerful bearing greatly encouraged them. She was in turn saluted with every demonstration of love, loyalty and obedience. At certain hours also, an eye-witness wrote, "Divers psalms, prayers and praises ascend to the Almighty from the camp of Tilbury, which the queen nowise misliked, but which she greatly commended, and with earnest speech thanked God with them."

The queen present. Cheers and animates the troops.

She is very popular and much loved and honoured.

She approves of worship in camp by the troops.

The soldiers appreciate and honour the presence of their queen.

The soldiers were quite delighted with and much admired the bearing of their sovereign, as, carrying a marshal's truncheon, she rode gallantly on a white charger among them, or at her tent received the knights and nobles who, proffering their services, flocked, with joyful demonstration, around her. She addressed her troops, sitting on her war horse, one rein of which was *The Earls of* held by the Earl of Leicester and the other by *Leicester and Essex* the Earl of Essex. Her famous and burning *each hold a rein of* speech stirred all hearts. She avowed, as she *her bridle while she de-* undoubtedly felt, ardent devotion to her king- *livers the following* dom and her people. The following are the *stirring speech to the* words of the queen's often-quoted address:— *army.*

"My loving people, we have been persuaded by some that are careful of our safety, to take heed how we commit ourselves to armed multitudes, for fear of treachery; but I assure you I do not desire to live to distrust my faithful, loving people. Let tyrants fear!

"I have always so behaved myself that, under God, I have placed my chiefest strength and safeguard in the loyal hearts and goodwill of my subjects; and therefore I am come amongst you, as you see, at this time, not for my recreation and disport, but being resolved, in the midst and heat of the battle, to live and die amongst you all; to lay down for my God, and for my kingdom, and for my people, my honour and my blood, even in the dust. I know I have the body of a weak and feeble woman, but I have the heart and stomach of a king, and of a King of England, too; and think foul scorn that Parma, or Spain, or any king of Europe, should dare to invade the borders of my realm! To which, rather than that any dishonour shall grow by me, I myself will take up arms—I myself will be your general, judge and rewarder of every one of your virtues in the field. I know already for your forwardness you have deserved rewards and crowns, and we do assure you, on the word of a prince, they shall be duly paid you.

"In the meantime, my Lieutenant-General shall be in my stead, than whom never prince commanded a more noble or worthy subject; not doubting but that by your obedience to my General, by your concord in the event, and your valour in the field, we shall shortly have a famous victory over those enemies of God, of my kingdom and of my people!"

Thus she fired the patriotism of the people and made hersel strong in their love, loyalty and devotion. Such strength was mightier, at such a time, than wealth, material resources or numbers. The army of the interior was also organized, and was composed of volunteers of different ranks and of every class. It consisted of thirty-six thousand foot, and was commanded, as already observed, by Lord Lunsden. It was meant for the double purpose—first, of defending the queen's person in case the invaders should pass Tilbury; and second, as a reserve force to move whenever and wherever most needed.

The queen aroused the patriotic feelings of her people and made herself secure in their affection.

It is but truth to say that, when the Armada appeared, this army existed only on paper. Nor did it attain to any fulness or efficiency at any time. When the danger passed, so, in large degree, did the enthusiasm, which for a short time inspired it. Happily, no invader made demand upon it for service. It is well, however, to observe that the more perfectly organized army at Tilbury was composed of men of all ranks and conditions in the country. The ploughman and farmer followed the landed proprietor to the

The army of the interior never fully organized.

The composition and spirit of the volunteers.

field—the apprentice and clerk the alderman of his ward—the tradesman and mechanic the employer. All willingly offered themselves and were gratefully accepted for whatever service they could best perform. No haughtiness or disrespect was shown by any one towards another, but feelings of amity and unity of aim and interest pervaded all. They were all English, were all beset with a common danger, and were all animated with the love of country, freedom, home and religion. This heritage they were determined to defend and transmit to those who should come after them.

Self-sacrificing and patriotic.

CHAPTER XIII.

THE KING OF SPAIN PRESCRIBES THE PLAN OF MOVEMENT.

The course of the Armada till joining with the army. Pass Cape Finisterre and through the Bay of Biscay.

THE order of movement to be observed by the Spanish fleet and army was laid down by King Phillip before the Armada set sail. He directed that, steering clear of the coasts of Spain, the fleet pass near as consistent with safety to Cape Finisterre, keep right on by a north and north-east course through the Bay of Biscay till entering the English Channel.

Steer near as safety allows to the coast of France.

After that to bear as near to the coast of France as the pilots judged safe until they reached the narrow sea off Calais, Dunkirk, Newport, or Gravelines. At some of these places to communicate with and await the movements of the Duke of Parma, whose army, mustered in Flanders, would now join them. Then, under protection of the Armada, they

Make a junction with Parma at Calais.

ENGLAND'S VICTORY OVER THE ARMADA.

would cross the Channel and enter the Thames. A landing of Parma's soldiers, together with six thousand troops from the Armada, to be made on the shores of Kent or Essex. He then desired this force to advance on London—one part of the Armada would then move toward the eastern coast, but the chief portion would take charge of all the water approaches along the southern coast, including especially those of Hampshire and Dorset. It was further arranged that the Duke of Guise, leader of the Holy League, with a small squadron, should effect a landing on some part of the western coast—Cornwall or Devon—to produce a diversion while the army of Parma was effecting the conquest of London and parts to the north.

The plan was known in England before the fleet arrived in the Channel. Hence a camp was formed at Tilbury in Essex, which was connected at Gravesend by a bridge of boats, which thus united the Essex and Kentish shores of the Thames.

Admiral Medina Sidonia was ready, the winds also favouring, to put to sea from Corunna on the 16th of July. He was led, as he drew near the English Channel, to depart a little from the instructions of his master, on receiving information from an English fisherman, whom he there captured. The prisoner informed him that the English, on hearing of the violent and disastrous storms which the Spanish fleet had encountered off their own coast, concluded that the attempt on England could not be renewed that year, and hence had laid up their ships at Plymouth and dismissed a large number of their sailors. This agreeable news disposed the Spanish admiral to strike out into the English Channel and bear directly for Plymouth, in hope of capturing or destroying the English fleet. He, however, mistook the Lizard for the Plymouth light, and so sailed for this more distant point. This error proved an advantage to the English admiral, for he got tidings of the approach of the Armada, and so gained time to prepare for his approach and thwart his design. A Scottish pirate, or sea-rover, named Fleming, having first seen the Armada, and observed it bearing toward the Lizard, hastened to bear the tidings to the English admiral. Though a fresh gale blew in their face at Plymouth docks, Howard that night roped out his ships into the roads, and promptly put all in readiness for sea. The Armada's mistake gave the English time to make these orderly movements, and rendered the designed capture or destruction of their fleet impossible. The invaders had their first view of the goodly land which Philip and Sextus the Fifth had promised them, and which they hoped soon to possess, on Friday, July the nineteenth, 1588. The same evening the Armada's approach was signalled along all the southern coast of England by the kindling of beacon fires on every height from Land's End to Margate. These blazing signals told all England that the menaced invasion of their country was now to be attempted.

On Saturday, the 20th day of July, about three o'clock in the afternoon, the drifting rains of the morning having cleared away, the English fleet got their first view of the great Armada from Plymouth roads. The great ships, galleons, galeases, galleys, and caravels of that vast armament, to the number of one hundred and sixty, spread over the Channel in the form of a crescent, whose horns were fully seven miles apart. So many ships, having such high decks, lofty masts, of such bulk and tonnage, all so well appointed and strongly manned and armed, spreading so widely its white wings, and moving with such stately majesty and seeming power, had never before been seen on those waters. It seemed a great pageant, prepared for scenic effect, rather than a work of conquest.

It is harvest time.

Thousands flock to the hilltops to see the spectacle.

Though it is the season of harvest, and the fertile fields of England are full of store, and call for many hands to reap them, yet the thousands of her industrial people for several days gather in crowds on every hill and upland along the coast, from the Lizard to the Start, beholding the vast and menacing spectacle.

This was the reptile age in the arts of shipbuilding and navigation. Those huge, clumsy, crawling monsters of the deep excited wonder among a people who had never seen the like. But in the present stage of those arts the fleet of the Invincible Armada is as great a curiosity to shipbuilders and seamen as a school of Ichthyosaurus or crocodiles to the geologist.

No engagement off Plymouth.

The dreaded Armada does not, however, steer for Plymouth, but shears off and keeps on her course eastward, the admiral now remembering his master's orders. His designs on Plymouth prove delusive, and are abandoned. His enemies are in possession, and before his eyes. Will our English admiral make the attack, and bring on an engagement? He is too astute for that. His fleet is not yet collected. He has only thirty-four ships. But many small squadrons will pour out from every port along the Channel, and swell his force.

How rapidly the tidings of the Armada's arrival in the Channel spread over all England is vividly described by Macaulay in the following verses:—

> "Such night in England ne'er hath been,
>   Nor e'er again shall be.
> From Eddystone to Berwick bounds,
>   From Lynn to Milford Bay,
> That time of slumber was as bright
>   And busy as the day;
> For swift to east and swift to west
>   The ghastly war-flame spread,
> High on St. Michael's Mount it shone;
>   It shone on Beechy Head.
> Far on the deep the Spaniard saw,
>   Along each southern shire,
> Cape beyond cape in endless range,
>   Those twinkling points of fire.
> The fisher left his skiff to rock
>   On Tamar's glittering waves;

The rugged miners poured to war
  From Mendip's sunless caves;
O'er Lougleat's towers, o'er Cranbourne's oaks
  The fiery herald flew;
He roused the shepherds of Stonehenge,
  The rangers of Beaulieu.
Right quick and sharp the bells all night
  Rang out from Bristol town,
And ere the day three hundred horse
  Had met at Clifton down;
The sentinel on Whitehall gate
  Looked forth into the night,
And saw o'erhanging Richmond Hall
  The streak of blood-red light.
Then bugle's note and cannon's roar
  The death-like silence broke,
And with one start, and with one cry,
  The royal city woke.
At once, on all her stately gates,
  Arose the answering fires;
At once the wild alarum clashed
  From all her ruling spires;
From all the batteries of the tower
  Pealed loud the voice of fear;
And all the thousand masts of Thames
  Sent back a louder cheer."

CHAPTER XIV.

THE STRUGGLE UP THE CHANNEL.

The fleets approach and survey each other.

ON the 21st of July, about nine in the morning, the fleets approached each other. The Captain-General, Medina Sidonia, stands in his shot-proof fortress on the deck of his flagship the "Saint Martin," with a full staff of Spanish grandees and military officers—generals, colonels and captains—most of whom know as little of naval warfare as the admiral himself. The English had many experienced and able captains, who felt quite *The English ships quick and rapid, the Spanish slow and clumsy.* at home on the water. Their ships, also, move with ease and alacrity; while the great ships of the Spaniard, which could, by their great weight, easily crush the English at close quarters, are clumsy and incapable of rapid or ready action.

With his gallant little fleet Howard approaches and surveys the giant Armada. In the spirit and might with which the stripling David long ago encountered the proud giant of the Philistines, he and his countrymen purpose to meet the proud fleet of the Armada. The English captains and seamen, who have before handled Spanish galleons, neither fear nor are dismayed. They become strong when they remember their homes, their queen, their liberties and religion, which are imperilled, and which are dearer to them than life. With God's help they will defend them to the last extremity with life, honour, and all their worldly resources. The English admiral ordered his pinnace, called the "Disdain," to give the Spanish admiral the defiance. The little craft fires a shot at random, in feudal fashion, at the first Spanish ship she meets. This is speedily followed by a lively cannonade from the admiral's ship, the "Ark Royal," on, as he supposed, the "Saint Martin," the Duke of Medina's flag-ship. The Spanish ships promptly responded. For a little while the scene is sharp and hot. The struggle has indeed begun.

The spirit of the English, like that of David in meeting Goliath.

The challenge given.

Promptly accepted.

The struggle begun.

The English admiral had, however, prudently ordered his captains to avoid being led into a

ENGLAND'S VICTORY OVER THE ARMADA.

The English decline a general engagement, but hang on and distress the Spanish.

general engagement, but cannonade the enemy at safe distance, to hang on his flanks and rear, and to distress him whenever they had opportunity. Drake and Hawkins kept up a brisk fire on the hindmost squadron, commanded by Admiral Recalde. In consequence of this his flagship was so battered and broken that she was hardly able to regain her place among the ships of the Armada.

The tactics and manœuvres of the English excel the Spanish.

The superior seamanship of the English was manifested in the first encounter. They, having at once secured the weather-gage, began to cannonade the enemy with considerable effect. Their active movements and skilful sallies, were in striking contrast to the sluggish tactics of their adversaries. For though the ships of the latter were of far greater weight, yet the former could deliver an action with so much greater point, and more speedily pass out of

The strength of the latter superior.

the reach of danger. The Spanish were compelled to admit, and did not fail to admire, their superior manœuvring.

The Armada keeps on her course after the first brush.

For two hours this trial of skill and strength lasted, and gave to both sides a foretaste of what each might expect from the other in the days of struggle soon to come. The Armada kept on her course, inclining a little more to the southward. The English, though their ships were still few in number, were encouraged by the ease with which they could work them, the quickness with which they could advance, tack, fire, and regain their position. The huge galleons made splendid marks for their fire, but were too heavy and large for active movements, besides their weight was such that the English seldom fell within the range of their guns, the shot passing harmlessly over their heads. They could approach, pour out a broadside and return before a galleon or galley could get their range or reach them.

They suffered much more damage than did the English.

The Spanish fought bravely, notwithstanding their disadvantage. Says Drake in a letter then written: "So far as we, see they mean to sell their lives with blows." The English fire told even in this first engagement. The Biscayan flagship, the "San Juan," had her mizzen-mast shot through, some of her spars carried away, her captain wounded and fifteen of her men killed. Oquendo, the commander of that squadron, showed great gallantry in that he carried into action those who flinched, and animated all to the highest daring. They

The Spanish fight bravely nevertheless.

failed to inflict any serious injury on the English.

A Guypuzcoan galley blown up by a Fleming.

A great galley was that day lost which belonged to the squadron of Guypuzcoa. One of her officers, who was a Fleming, took mortal offence at the reprimand that morning administered to him by his captain, and determined to avenge his wrong. Taking a fuse-match, he secretly set it to the magazine of the ship, and, unobserved, kindled it. Immediately after he leaped into the sea. In an instant a terrible explosion is heard. The whole upper decks of the ship were torn up, some two hundred men killed, and the ship set on fire. The paymaster of the squadron was among those who perished. By great effort the flames were quenched, and those surviving were transferred to other ships. The English, who saw the burning ship, hastened to capture her. She was found to contain considerable powder and military stores, which proved of value in replenishing the too scanty stores at the disposal of the English.

200 lives lost in her.

Military stores gained by the English.

On Monday, the 22nd of July, the Spanish admiral made important changes in the relative positions of certain squadrons of his fleet. He himself led the van. He placed Vice-Ad-

De Leyva put in charge of the rear squadron.

miral Don Antonio de Leyva in the rear with a squadron of forty-three large ships. He instructed him to deal vigilantly with the English, who were harassing their rear, and bring

To try and bring an engagement at close quarters.

them to an engagement at close quarters as speedily as possible. On their part the English soon proved to his satisfaction that they, not he, were masters of the situation, and could choose or refuse a general engagement, just as they pleased. They would not, however, readily enter such an engagement, as they were instructed not to fall into any such trap.

The Duke of Medina issues two despatches, one to the Duke of Parma.

The Duke of Medina issued two other despatches—one to the Duke of Parma, by Juan Gil in a sloop, informing the duke of his approach, stating he had not yet found the English inclined to risk a formal engagement, that he wished him to send him some pilots who knew the Channel, for in case of a storm he did not know where he would find shelter, and craving information as to the time and place of meeting.

The second despatch directs the hanging of any officer who leaves his position.

The other despatch was to his fleet for the purpose of promoting discipline. He sent a sergeant-major with written instructions to every ship in the Armada to hang any officer.

without appeal or consultation, who should leave the position assigned him; and to ensure the observance of his orders he sent hangmen with the bearer of the despatch. We are not informed how far the threat promoted good order.

The English fleet rapidly increased as it passed along the Channel.

On the twenty-third, Sir Walter Raleigh, with a small squadron, joined the fleet, which was off Portland. Many other nobles, merchants and gentry poured out from every port along the Channel, each adding his contingent to the fleet. For the news had now spread over all England that the "Invincible Armada" was in the Channel and hotly pressing the English admiral every day.

The tide of patriotism rises high, and for the time internal bickerings cease.

Patriotism fired the heart of England in the face of subjugation to the intolerant King of Spain. Religious bickerings and sectarian strife were for the time laid aside, except by the Jesuits and their young converts, with the extreme Romanists, as Allen and Parsons, and that ilk. Even the young Percies, Cliffords, and De Veres joined Howard's fleet and united with their Protestant countrymen in swelling his naval force so that it now reached its fullest dimensions. It was now equal to the Spanish, at least in number, and Admiral Medina was surprised at the growing force with which he had to contend. The unanimity and presence of all classes and parties in the fleet gave new power and courage to the seamen, so that each became a hero, resolved to show himself worthy of the respect of his country. The Armada was not far from the English fleet off Portland. Drake and Frobisher, who were ever watching for an opportunity to strike a blow, were in the same (the rear) division of the English fleet, over against the hindermost squadrons of the Armada. A heavy cannonade was opened on these squadrons, which the Spanish encouraged, desiring greatly to draw the English into an engagement alongsides and at close quarters. This the latter wisely avoided, because the advantage in such cases was always with the heavier over the lighter ships. But the English kept tacking about from side to side, suddenly making sallies in upon the large ships, pouring in a broadside and quickly sheering off again. Thus by their nimble movements they galled the Spanish, who in their sluggish ships could seldom strike them, or even find their range, till they were

Marginalia:
- The seamen become heroes.
- The English rear squadrons opposite the Spanish rear.
- The former avoid, the latter encourage, coming to close quarters

gone. They kept up this mode of desultory attack so systematically that Sir Henry Wooton, who saw them practise these tactics, compared their movements to a morris-dance upon the waters, so light, nimble and orderly were their manœuvres.*

Sir Henry Wooton's remarks on the English tactics.

On that day of successful experiment and during enterprise, Drake and Frobisher took valuable prizes, *i.e.*, the flagship of Don Pedro de Valdez, commander of the Andalusian

A valuable prize taken.

---

* Sir Walter Raleigh, an eye-witness and participator in the struggle with the Armada, highly approved of Admiral Howard's prudence and skill in not allowing the English fleet to fight the Spanish at close quarters. Says he: "There is more belonging to a good man-of-war upon the waters than great daring. There is a great deal of difference between fighting loose, or at large, and grappling. The guns of a slow ship pierce as well, and make as great holes, as those in a swift. To clap ships together, without consideration, belongs rather to a madman than a man-of-war. The Lord Admiral Howard had lost in 1588 had he not been better advised than to follow such mad course. The Spaniards had an army aboard them and he had none; they had more ships than he had, and of higher building and charging, so that, had he entangled himself with those great and powerful vessels, he had greatly endangered this kingdom of England. For twenty men upon the defences are equal to a hundred that board and enter; whereas, then, contrariwise, the Spaniards had a hundred for twenty of ours to defend themselves with. But our admiral knew his advantage, and held it, which had he not done, he had not been worthy to have held his head."

squadron. The mainmast of the ship "Catalonia" having been broken two days before, had in falling torn down and broken much of the gear and tackle of his ship, so that she fell behind, unable to make much speed. The admiral ordered two large ships to take her in tow, but so heavy was the sea that the cables broke, and she was left for the night. The part of the English fleet nearest to her, in command of Drake and Frobisher, observing her condition in the morning, encountered her. After a brief resistance she struck to Drake. He took her with him into Torbay, carried Valdez and the officers with him, but left the ship and men at Torbay in charge of the people. This valuable prize had four hundred and fifty men and officers, with the commander of a squadron, and considerable treasure. The money taken was distributed among the sailors of the ships making the capture. The ransom of the admiral went to the officer who ordered the capture.

Don Pedro de Valdez and his ship taken by Drake and Frobisher.

The ship and 450 officers and men go to Torbay.

The money distributed among the sailors.

Drake gets the ranson of Valdez.

Frobisher engages Recalde.

The gallant Frobisher and his noble ship the "Triumph," followed by five merchantmen, were drawn into close quarters with part of Recalde's squadron. A desperate fight, which lasted

Howard comes to his aid.

more than two hours, ensued. Admiral Howard, seeing the odds with which Frobisher was bravely contending, signalled part of his own squadron to move to his relief. He also ordered a few of the lighter craft to tow him out. All were safely drawn off, while still pouring in effective showers of shot on their sturdy adversary.

A Venetian argosy and transports taken.

A Venetian argosy and several transports were taken by the English and sent into the port of Weymouth. Being still short of powder, and wishing to avoid a general engagement, and also desirous of changing their relative positions, the English early that morning put out to sea to secure again the weather-gage. The Spanish supposed they were escaping an engagement with them through fear, and began to pursue, but their ships, save a very few,

The "St. Mark" gives chase.

made little headway. One, the "St. Mark," ran ahead of all the fleet, and soon stood out several miles from the rest of the Armada. The English, feeling bound to disable as many ships as they possibly could, and so weaken their adversary's power, turned on the "St. Mark," and for more than an hour they poured a heavy fire, both of small and large shot, into her.

The "St. Mark" rescued by Oquendo. Darkness closes up a day of toil and danger.

She fought gallantly, and successfully defended herself till Oquendo, coming to her relief, rescued her. Darkness at length began to fall on the sounds of the guns, and brought the strife of that busy day to a close. Many of the Spanish ships were crippled; not one of the English were noticeably injured.

The day following was more quiet, and proved a prelude to another day of stirring scenes and bloody strife. The twenty-fifth of July is St. James' Day, the patron saint of Spain, to whose honour the day is consecrated in the Roman calendar. Will the saint smile auspiciously on his devotees? On this day of peril will he help them in their struggles? The Spaniard does not seem eager to put his favour to the test, or to invoke the protection of his ægis. The occasion, however, soon arrives.

The 25th of July, St. James' Day, the patron saint of Spain.

The English have received supplies of powder sufficient for one day's fighting, and still greater reinforcements to their fleet from the several ports of Dorset and Hampshire, off which shires they now lie. They are at their best, and number a hundred and forty to fifty sail. A transport, the "Santana," and a Portuguese galleon, having been somewhat crippled two days

Off Portland on St. James' Day.

before, fell behind the Armada. Frobisher, in his flagship, the "Triumph," with a few others, proceeded to capture and bring them in. Soon as his design is seen, three great galleons, moved by a thousand oars, dispute his claim, and proceed to chasten him for his daring. At once four or five of the queen's ships open fire upon them. The "Golden Lion," the "White Bear," the "Elizabeth," and the "Leicester," bear down into the midst of the Spanish fleet. They pour in tons of heavy shot upon the Spaniards, until, it is said, "the blood ran out a scupper hole." The wind favouring, Howard bears down on the "St. Martin," Admiral Medina's flagship. The fighting became almost general. The mainmast of the "St. Martin" was shot away. His ship was disabled, and was about to strike to Frobisher. He was, however, promptly rescued by his brave captains, Mexica and Recalde, who threw themselves between the commander and his enemy, and so saved him the mortification of surrendering his ship. Oquendo, who was always in the hottest of the strife, strove to retaliate on Admiral Howard, and threw himself across the "Ark Royal," thinking to disable her. The

"Ark," however, ran into his ship, and two of his soldiers at the forecastle were killed by the shock. The "Ark's" rudder was displaced, so she was for a time unmanageable. She cleared herself of Oquendo's ship and fell a little to the leeward. A fierce and prolonged struggle ensues. Howard directs and animates his men, who act with great coolness and presence of mind. They have now begun work in earnest. The two fleets are nearly yardarm to yardarm. Broadside after broadside from the great guns, volley after volley of arquebuses from deck to mainmast and rigging, were hotly exchanged. Much greater damage was inflicted on the Spanish than was received by the English ships. For the former made an easy mark, while the shot from their high turrets passed almost harmlessly over the heads of the English. The Spanish admiral wished to bring the English to engage at close quarters; the latter wisely evaded such a mad experiment. Frobisher for a time plunged into close contact, and but for timely aid might have precipitated a terrible battle. But he and all the English behaved with such gallantry that the admiral was more than satisfied. There was a gen-

Marginal notes:
- A fierce fight long continued.
- The two fleets in close conflict for a while.
- The English have the advantage.

eral feeling of confidence and cheerful anticipations of future success, as Admiral Howard withdrew the "Ark Royal," followed by the rest of his ships, from further action. English courage and gallantry were conspicuous all that day. Nothing decisive, it is true, was accomplished; but the English had come off safely, for hardly a man had been wounded, and none killed. They had not made any prizes. They retained, it is likely, the transports they had captured in the morning, but had expended much of their munition. Though the effects were not visible, they were real and abiding. The English balls tore up the heavy timbers and turrets of the Spanish galleons, and sent splinters of their timbers flying like shells among the men who had been sent for safety below. The rigging, also arms, masts, etc., were badly torn. There were many men wounded, and a considerable number killed. Instead of settling the contest by one great battle, the Spanish found that they must fight every day, and no cheering hope before them of a successful issue. Their stores of powder and shot, which they had no ready way of renewing, were falling low, and the sense of

Medina writes to Parma.

insecurity was increasing. That very day Medina wrote to Parma, "The enemy pursues me. They fire upon me most days from morning to night, but they will not grapple with us. I have given them every opportunity, but they

Medina apprehensive and in straits.

decline to accept. There is no remedy for us, because they are swift and we are slow. They have men and ammunition in abundance, while their action has almost exhausted ours; and if their coolness last, and they continue the same tactics, as they assuredly will, I must request your excellency to send me two shiploads of shot and powder immediately. I am in urgent need of it."

On the next day all was quiet on both fleets. Even the sea was calm and unruffled. The Spaniards move toward Boulogne, on the coast of France; the English toward Dover, for supplies, of which they were in great need. Howard gathered many of the heroes of the day before around him, and bestowed on them the

Admiral Howard knights several of his heroes of the 25th.

honours of knighthood. Among those so distinguished are Martin Frobisher, John Hawkins, and Roger Townsend. The English now possessed comfortable proof that the Armada was not invincible; for, while their own fleet had greatly increased, it had considerably decreased. They had lost already quite a number of their proudest ships. Both fleets hold on their course. The English admiral gave orders to his captains not to renew the fight till they had come into the narrow sea between Dover and Calais.

All is quiet till reaching the waters of Dover and Calais.

CHAPTER XV.

THE STRUGGLE OFF CALAIS.

Arrive at Calais on July 27th.

ON the evening of Saturday, the 27th of July, the Armada reached Calais Roads and speedily cast anchor. It had come as near to the camp of Parma as was possible for it. Parma still lay in Flanders with his great army of invasion, willing, but still unable, to move.

No signs of the Duke of Parma. No letters for the admiral of the Armada.

Admiral Medina seemed to expect to meet the duke with his troops all waiting to join him and ready at once to cross the Channel into England. In this he was disappointed, and more reasonably that he did not find even a line in answer to his several letters and requests.

He writes to Parma.

He wrote again on the evening of his arrival (*i.e.*, the 27th July) at Calais. He requested thirty or forty fly-boats or gun-boats which could move quickly and keep the English at bay, which his slow and heavy vessels could not do. He also expressed anxiety, if he should be long delayed, to secure a more safe place of anchorage than that of Calais Roads.

The difficulties of the Duke of Parma.

The Duke of Parma had his own difficulties. He lacked both money and stores of food. His troops had not been paid; neither had they been adequately victualled; and were on the point of mutiny and famine. He had kept his troops together by promises and assurances that supplies were coming with the fleet.

He cannot reach Medina without protection.

They were ready to embark with their transports, but could not get out into the sea, because all the passages were guarded with armed ships, and his vessels were nearly all flat-bottomed transports without armament. He expected the admiral to open the way and protect him in the passage across the Channel. He could not send gun-boats, because he had none. He would provide, "as far as his poverty would allow," ammunition; but must trust to the admiral of the Armada for protection.

The fleet in helpless and disheartening condition.

Thus the grand fleet of invasion and conquest has arrived at the scene of action so helpless that she begins by begging assistance.

The grand army of co-operation is unable to join the navy, as the navy is to extend its protecting arms to the army.

The English fleet in between the Armada and Dover.

The English fleet, which followed closely on the Spanish, took position in the Channel some two miles west and north of the Armada, toward Dover. The hours of that Saturday night and the following Sabbath-day were hours

A critical moment is that in England.

of great solicitude and peril to England. For in sight of her shores, only a few miles distant from the entrance of the Thames, lay the "Invincible Armada" waiting to co-operate with the famous army and the most able commander of

All is at stake.

Spain, in conquering England. Within two short miles of that Armada lies the marvellously vigilant and daring little fleet of England ready to venture everything which courage, honour or manhood might, for queen and country. This is under God England's main hope of successful resistance to her enemies and the protection of her coasts. No resource of generous courage or daring, no hour of precious time must be lost, but turned, and that without delay, to the best account.

It is now clear what the crafty, dissimulating little old man of the Escorial meant by the peace

ENGLAND'S VICTORY OVER THE ARMADA. 131

False pretences of peace negotiations.

negotiations, carried on through his generalissimo in Flanders, up to the last moment. The Queen of England wanted peace, and would hear of nothing else. The people of England—the statesmen and patriots—wanted freedom, independence and honour, if with peace well, but if with war, then were they for war. Every Englishman then saw that the moment had come for striking the most telling blows possible. They must fall thick and fast, until the foe yields and England is free. She will not pause till the last ball has been shot, the last ship sunk, the last arm become powerless, and the last hope has perished. No one, however, felt that such a day was near.

England resolute and uncompromising.

Sabbath the 28th July a sacred and momentous day.

That Sabbath was a day on which the heart of England beat with devout and Christian, as with patriotic emotion and solicitude. Earnest prayer ascended to God from every Protestant church, from every Christian family and heart in the land. The cry of all to God was, "Save and deliver us, we humbly beseech Thee, from the hand of our enemies."

A day of humble prayer and devout trust in God.

All truthful historians give us a pleasing picture of the spirit of true piety and humble prayer which pervaded England. Queen and

The queen indites a prayer which is sent to the army.

people, Churchman and Puritan, every Christian, was earnestly calling on God in hearty accord with every other. The queen herself composed a prayer, which was sent to the army that it might stimulate the men to, as well as to guide them in, prayer. It is not, certainly, lacking in either earnestness or trust in God, even if it is a little peremptory in its requests. It is entitled

Queen Elizabeth's prayer or private meditation:

"Most Omnipotent, and Guider of all our world's mass, that only searchest and fathomest the bottom of all hearts, conceits, and in them seest the true original of all actions intended, how no malice of revenge, nor quittance of injury, nor desire for bloodshed, nor greediness of lucre hath bred the resolution of our now set-out army; but a heedful care, and wary watch, that no neglect of foes, nor over surety of harm, might breed either danger to us, or glory to them. These being grounds, Thou that didst inspire the wind, we humbly beseech, with bended knees, prosper the work, and with the best forewinds guide the journey, speed the victory, and make the return the advancement of Thy glory, the triumph of Thy fame, and surety to the realm, with the least loss of

ENGLAND'S VICTORY OVER THE ARMADA. 133

English blood. To these devout petitions, Lord, give Thou Thy blessed grant." *Amen.*

Lord Seymour comes with part of his squadron to Calais.
Lord Henry Seymour, who, with a squadron of forty Dutch and English ships, lay off the Flemish coast guarding its harbours and watching the movements of the Duke of Parma's army, to prevent its getting out into the Channel from Gravelines, Dunkirk, Newport, or Antwerp by the Scheldt, now joins the English with part of his squadron.

A council of war held.
In the evening a council of war was held on board the "Ark Royal," Lord Howard's ship. There assembled Seymour, Drake, Sheffield, Southwell, Palmer, Hawkins, Winter, Fenner and Frobisher, Lord Howard presiding. The decision and subsequent actions of that council determined the fate of England. The minds of all were fixed on taking immediate action.

Some things to be prevented.
The Duke of Medina must not have time, all agreed, given him to form new combinations or arrange new plans of action. The Spanish fleet must be further crippled, if not destroyed, and this without delay. For if by any means a junction of the Spanish army is made with the Armada, the hardships of England will be the greater.

Plan to produce a panic among the Spanish.

The council, knowing the shallowness of the shoals off the coast east of the Armada, also how much the Spanish dreaded fire-ships, and believing good would come of throwing the whole fleet into a panic in the coming night, determined

Fire-ships employed to create panic.

to take eight of the smaller ships, of which there was no need, and, smearing them with pitch, and filling them with tar, resin, dried wood and all sorts of combustible materials, towing them out in the darkness, turn them into the lines of the Spanish fleet. Then when near enough, set them all at once on fire, leaving them to float in among the Spanish ships.

The ships let loose about 2 a.m.

About two o'clock of Monday morning, the 29th of July, the night being dark and cloudy, and the tide flowing strongly from the English to the French coast, when the Armada was closely gathered in the shelter of the coast, and

Are borne by the tide and winds among the Spanish ships.

the winds also favouring, the eight ships were towed down; when near the Spanish lines they were suddenly lighted, and left to float among the ships of the Armada.

The great surprise and singularly flaring light.

Immediately sheets of fire burst out from every one of them; volumes of sulphurous smoke and lurid flame filled the air. The singular brightness revealed the towers, forts, and church spires of Calais. The inhabitants of Dover and the coast of Kent gazed in wonder at the glare of light. The Spanish soldiers and seamen were all wrapped in slumber, save a few on the watch, who saw through the darkness shadowy objects moving toward them, but were uncertain whether any substantial thing were approaching them, till a pyramid of flame and lurid light flashed from sail to sail and over forecastles, masts, and yards. The alarm was raised. All were panic-struck. They thought that some diabolical engine of destruction had come among them. Many of the Spaniards remembered the destruction wrought at Antwerp in 1585 by the wild-fire which made such havoc of Parma's men, as well as of his great bridge. They raised the cry, "Fire of Antwerp!" "Fire of Antwerp!!"

The panic spread through the entire fleet! The galleons lying at anchor had each cast two, and few had provided a third. The signal came from the "St. Martin" to make for sea. Many cut their cables and let their ships drive! Others slipped their hawsers! All broke with greatest haste, trying to escape the terrible calamity, and fled, they knew not whither.

Injury to the ships.

Some of the largest ships struck against and damaged others near them; others again were driven into shallows, or on the sands of the Flemish coast. Many drifted up the Channel before the wind, and when the morning light shone on them they were off the harbour of Gravelines—two leagues from Calais. Most of the ships were but slightly injured, and intended to return to their former positions, pick up their anchors, and wait till hearing further from the Duke of Parma.

Most of the ships off Gravelines when morning came.

The admiral meant they should return to their former stations.

But the confusion and disorder were general throughout the fleet. This the English desired and had managed to bring about. Now they wish to turn it to good account. Drake, with half the fleet, stood out into the Channel, hanging on the Spaniards' skirts. Howard, with the remainder, hovered about near Calais, hoping to drive the slowest on the sands or shallows. No time was given the enemy to rearrange their ships, or form new combinations.

The English wished to strike, while the confusion lasts, such as had not run ashore.

One of the largest galleons, the "Capitana," having De Monçada on board, had stranded on the bar of Calais. She had her helm displaced, and became unmanageable in the panic, and the ebbin tide had carried her ashore and left her

The "Capitana" on the bar of Calais.

ENGLAND'S VICTORY OVER THE ARMADA.

in sand and shallow water within range of the French batteries. Howard wished to make sure of her, that she would no longer be available for sea-fighting.

In capturing her a furious and bloody fight was made, for she was well manned and equipped, having of soldiers, sailors and galley-slaves, seven hundred men. Several hundred of these were slain in the contest for mastery; also a few English sailors. The galley-slaves, striking for liberty, sprang overboard, some swam and some waded to shore, a few of them were drowned. The English sailors climbed up over the bulwarks, boarding the ship; several of them falling in the attempt. They claimed her, and tried to remove her, but were arrested in the effort by the Governor of the Fort of Calais, who claimed the ship as lying under his guns. He, however, allowed the English seamen all the spoil, because of their gallant conduct in boarding her. There were fifty thousand gold ducats found on board, which the captors retained and distributed among themselves as prize-money.

CHAPTER XVI.

THE BATTLE OF GRAVELINES.

The Armada, off Gravelines, is pressed by the English.

DRAKE, whose comprehensive mind took in the advantages of the situation, had early taken his position with Seymour to prevent Medina from ever returning to his anchors. He was soon joined by Frobisher Hawkins, the lord-admiral and the rest. They purposed to keep the Spaniard in the dangerous seas and shallows all along the coast eastward, and not allow him, now that the rising gale favours their design, to escape from its power. The struggle of the day and of the hour culminates off Gravelines.

Seymour opens the battle with skill and courage.

Seymour, who had skill, courage and experience, opened the battle by a cannonade on the ships of the Spanish right. He reserved his not too-plentiful shot till within a hundred and twenty yards of the enemy, then poured it in showers, which continued all the fore noon from all the ships. The Spanish were driven in upon their own centre in a confused and entangled mass. The English spared no strokes they could bestow, but kept up a perpetual thunder of deadly and disabling fire from their guns at every point. It is said Sir William Winter delivered five hundred shot while he was all the time within range of their arquebuses, and sometimes within speaking distance of them.

The Spanish gun service was slow, clumsily performed, and remarkably ineffective. Their guns, worked on rolling carriages, or platforms, sent the shot sometimes into the air, sometimes into the water, according to the roll of the sea, and seldom struck their adversaries. Their ammunition was also, it was afterwards found, well-nigh spent, and partly accounted for the slowness of the service. The English, who had been pouring in shot upon them at some point or other from eight in the morning till five in the evening, paused when all were exhausted with labour, and almost the last cartridge spent. They had not waited on this day to take prizes, but

The Spanish driven into close quarters, and pressed in their confusion.

The English strike heavily and incessantly.

The Spanish gun-service very slow and poor.

Their ammunition also scarce.

The English pause at evening, when almost the last cartridge is gone and the enemy beaten.

aimed at disabling or destroying every ship they could.

Drake in the hot of the fight all day. Admiral Drake, whose judgment and daring were alike conspicuous, boldly encountered the foremost commanders of the Armada. With his brave ship the "Victory," he bore against Admiral Medina on the "St. Martin," the Rear-Admiral De Leyva on the "Rata,"

He encounters Medina, Oquendo, and other Spaniards. Oquendo, and others, who fought gallantly, and strove to preserve some degree of good order in the ships under their command. The winds beating on their high ships often exposed their windward sides below the water-line to the fire of the enemy, so that the great timbers, which were meant to be a protection

The English shot tells with great effect on the galleons even below the water-line. only increased the danger. For they were torn to pieces by the shot and the splinters driven with fatal effects among the men below—mid-decks thus became a very slaughter-house, where blood flowed in streams. Their guns, also, were dismantled, and the carpenters could hardly cover the holes and stop the leaks fast enough to keep the ships from sinking.

A galleon sunk. A large galleon of Biscay was sunk by the heavy fire poured into her in the morning. A few of her crew, who escape, tell a sad tale of desperate deeds done on her before she sank:

Horrors on board as she sank. Her chief officer, seeing the ship's condition, proposed to surrender her, and was instantly shot by a fellow-officer for daring to make such proposal. That officer's brother, in another instant, takes revenge on the murderer by plunging his poniard into his heart. The spirit of internecine desperation spreads, and other crimes as black are being committed, when the ship goes to the bottom, and all perish save these few who tell the tale.

On that Monday the "St. Mary," also with all on board, went down about the setting of the sun, not one escaping to tell the sad tale.

The "St. Matthew." The "Saint Matthew," a great Neapolitan ship, attempting to cover one of her comrades, which was in danger, is swept by the "Rainbow" and the "Vanguard." A brave Dutch ship follows with a heavy broadside. *Surrendering.* She is compelled to surrender. Another Spanish ship, a galleon *A Portugal galleon dismantled and captured.* of Portugal, is dismantled, and so, becoming unable to escape her pursuers, is captured. The wind and tides favour the English, whose fire tells upon the Spanish at many points.

The admiral finds his ships unmanageable, and many of his men dazed and bewildered.

The "St. Philip" sinking.
Another great galleon, the "St. Philip," commanded by Don Francisco, being badly crippled seemed to be about to sink. An English officer, seeing her condition, called from his forecastle to her commander, to surrender and so save life. A Spaniard instantly replied with a musket ball, which laid the officer lifeless on his own deck. The English ship bore away leaving them to their fate, while the scornful cry followed them from the sinking ship—"Cowardly heretics!" "Lutheran hens!!" "We dare you to engage us!!"

Called to surrender and save the lives of her men.

Spanish bravado.

The men and the rescuing ship all drowned.
This bravado was soon stopped by the sinking ship signalling for relief to a sister ship. The relieving ship in leaving the "St. Philip," received such a raking fire as disabled her, and before she had borne the men of the sinking ship out of danger, she herself went down. The "St. Philip" was left to drift and at length floated into Newport roads, giving no more trouble to the English. Many vessels of smaller size perished under the rain of shot which fell upon them. Others were riddled through and through, and several sunk.

Many transports and smaller ships disabled or sunk, others pierced by shots are unsafe; yet others perish.

ENGLAND'S VICTORY OVER THE ARMADA.

More than four thousand Spaniards were slain in the battle of Gravelines, and not more than one hundred English, most of whom had perished in the struggle for the "Capitana" on the bar of Calais. It is averred that not an English ship was lost; a few were, however, considerably disabled.

All the great Spanish ships which survived this furious storm of cannon balls were literally riddled, their masts and yards shattered, their sails and rigging torn to shreds. Thus as the decisive day advanced, the great Armada was rapidly becoming disabled. Admiral Medina tried to rally his men, keep his ships in line, and cheer on the soldiers. But they became disheartened. Everything seemed to conspire to bring about their defeat. The winds blew so stiff a breeze from the S. and S. W., in the afternoon, that the ships could not keep their place, but were driven out of line, up the Channel, on to the sands, or against their enemies. The anchors and cables of many of them had been lost the night before, and the sails of others had been terribly rent and torn.

Unfortunately for the English when all was going on so favourably for them, they found

The men become disheartened.

Even the winds against them.

Spanish ships cannot hold their places in line.

English successful, but their ammunition fails. their stores of ammunition beginning to fail. They were, therefore, compelled to use what remained sparingly at the very time when an abundant supply would have enabled them to have closed the most glorious day in England's naval history, with the complete destruction or certain surrender of the whole Spanish fleet.

Howard's stalwarts. They, however, did the best they possibly could. On the next day Admiral Howard, sending a despatch to Minister Walshingham, wrote, "Their force is wonderful, great and strong, and yet we pluck their feathers by little and little." He wrote a little later, "Notwithstanding that our powder and shot was well nearly all spent, we set on a brave countenance, and gave them chase, as though we wanted nothing, until we had cleared our own coasts and part of Scotland."

Two results reached of great value. Two important results were now achieved by the furious and prolonged contest of the 29th of July. First, the Armada was thoroughly crippled and no longer inspired terror as an "invincible" power; and second, the Duke of Parma could no longer hope to form a junction with the Armada and pass under its protection into England. The plan and purpose of the

The junction of Parma's army made impossible.

armament was, therefore, completely defeated. These were grand results. The English were then too thickly enveloped in the heat and smoke of the conflict to clearly see them, as they soon after did.

The battle, which lasted from eight in the morning to five or six in the evening, was fierce, destructive and unremitting. There were Spaniards fighting in the Armada, who had also participated in the memorable action of Lepanto, in the Levant, who affirmed that this day's fight off Gravelines far exceeded in severity that famous encounter. Nor would the conflict have slacked on the English side had not their stores of ammunition failed. But finding their munitions, their powder and shot, almost spent, they were compelled to slacken the fight and make out as best they could.

<small>The battle of Gravelines more severe than the encounter of Lepanto.</small>

The Spanish admiral, finding his ships crippled and broken, his ship-tackle, sails, cables and anchors gone, and pressed by a strong south-west wind so that he could no longer hold his position, is forced to think of how he may best escape with what remains of the Armada. He loses hope of uniting with the Duke of Parma, and protecting him across

<small>The state of the Spanish Armada after the battle.</small>

<small>Fears of Parma's treachery.</small>

the Channel. He suspects Parma of treachery, in leaving him to the worst in these shallows and dangerous seas. He will hold a council of war when the light of the next day shines.

We quote a few sentences from a contemporary writer, who graphically describes this last battle of the struggle off Gravelines. We give his words in their original quaintness of spelling and diction, as follows :—

"Upon the twenty-ninth of July, in the morning, the Spanish fleet, after the forsayd tumult (*i.e.*, from the fire-ships), having arranged themsuels againe into order, were within sight of Greveling, most bravely and furiously encountered by the English, where they once againe got the wind of the Spaniards, who suffered themselves to be deprived of the commodity of the place in Calais Roads, and of the advantage of the winds near unto Dunkirk, rather than they would change their array or separate their forces now conjoined and united together, standing only upon their defence.

"And howbeit there were many excellent and warlike ships in the English fleet, yet scarce were there twenty-two or twenty-three among them all, which matched ninety of the Spanish ships in bigness, or could conveniently assault them. Wherefore the English ships, using their prerogative of nimble steerage, whereby they could turn and wield themselves with the wind, which way they listed, came oftentimes very near upon the Spaniards, and charged them so sore that now and then they were but a pike's length asunder; and so continually giving them one broadside after another, they discharged all their shot, both great and small, upon them, spending one whole day, from morning till night, in that violent kind of conflict, untill such time as powder and bullets failed them. In regard of which want they thought it convenient not to pursue the Spaniards any longer, because they had many great vantages of the English, namely, for the extraordinary bigness of their ships, and also for that they were so neerly conjoined, and kept together in so good array, that they could by no means be fought withall one to one. The English thought, therefore, that they had right well acquited themselves in chasing the Spaniards first from Calais and then from Dunkirk, and by that means to have hindered them from joining with the Duke of Parma, his forces, and getting the wind of them, to have driven them from their own coasts."*

On Tuesday, the thirtieth of July, as the light of the sun began to shine, the scattered Armada saw the English following in the distance. It is St. Laurance's Day, Philip's patron saint. The king has, as he thinks, enriched the reliquary of the Escorial with a veritable bone of the saint. Will he be protected, as he believes, from all ills on that day by his favourite saint? Alas! the dead saint seems not to concern himself about the dangers of living sinners. Before them were the shallow seas of the Dutch coast, over which angry waves were breaking at mountain height. Behind were their enemies, faint, like Gideon's braves, yet pursuing. The Spanish ships are in great peril. They cannot anchor, because these are left behind at Calais. They cannot turn on their enemies and risk another battle, for they have no ammunition. If they go forward, the sea, which is becoming shallower every mile,

marginalia: St. Laurance's Day, Philip's patron saint. Has one of his bones. Will he help?

marginalia: Their dangers.

---

*Hakluyt, Vol. I, p. 602.

ENGLAND'S VICTORY OVER THE ARMADA. 149

will surely soon swallow them. Shall they surrender? for that alone gives hope of relief or safety.

The courses which open to them.

Happily for the Spanish, the peril of their situation is partly removed by a shifting of the wind to the south, which bears them off the breakers into the open sea. Now they must consider "what is to be done." Will they rally the Armada and make again for Calais, or will they pursue their course up the North seas?

They deliberate.

The Spanish hold a council of war.

A council of war is called. Recalde, De Leyva, Diego Flores, Caso Calderon, and the admiral, Medina, meet and deliberate. They see they cannot return to Calais as they wished, because both of the adverse winds and the English ships. The great enterprise for the present has to be given up. Parma must remain in Flanders. They decide to continue their course into the North Sea; they can then return to Spain by the Orkneys, the west of Ireland, and through the Atlantic. This, notwithstanding the roughness of the seas, the dangers of the islands, and hardships to be anticipated, is decided to be the safest and best, if not the only way open to them.

Decide to return to Spain by the North Sea, the Orkneys and west of Ireland.

The English admirals also held a council on

The English also hold a council. the same day. They did not yet know how greatly the Spanish had suffered, or how completely exhausted were their ammunition and supplies, and so expected a renewal of the fight as soon as the Spanish had a little time to rally. It was therefore decided that Lord Seymour, with thirty ships, should return to *Determine to watch Parma and the Armada as well.* the Flemish coast to watch the Duke of Parma, and that the remainder of the fleet of some ninety sail should follow and deal with the Armada. At night, that he might not be seen by the Spanish, Seymour, though his men were almost famished, and he longed to continue the pursuit of the Armada, made his way round the Brill and returned to his watch.

The 31st of July still following the Armada. On the 31st of July all the English fleet, saving Lord Seymour's squadron, which had departed in the night, kept in sight of the Spanish. As yet there is no disposition to give up the pursuit, nor belief that the struggle with the Armada is over. Drake wrote on this very day, the 31st July, to Walshingham in his own peculiar style:—

"We have the army of Spain before us, and mind, with the grace of God, to wrestle a fall with them. There was never anything pleased me better, than seeing the enemy flying with a south wind toward the northward. God grant they have a good eye to the Duke of Parma; for with the grace of God, if we live, I doubt it not but ere it be long, so to handle the matter with the Duke of Sidonia, as he shall wish himself at St. Marie's among his orange trees."

Mr. Green gives the following comprehensive view of the struggle of that memorable day:—

"At dawn the English ships closed fairly in, and almost their last cartridge was spent ere the sun went down. Three great galleons had sunk, three had drifted helplessly on the Flemish coast; but the bulk of the Spanish vessels remained, and even to Drake the fleet seemed 'wonderful, great and strong.' Within the Armada itself, however, all hope was gone. Huddled together by the wind and the deadly English fire, their sails torn, their masts shot away, the crowded galleons had become mere slaughter-houses. Four thousand men had fallen, and bravely as the seamen fought, they were cowed by the terrible butchery. Medina himself was in despair. 'We are lost, Señor

Oquendo,' he cried to his bravest captain, 'What are we to do?' 'Let others talk o being lost,' replied Oquendo. 'Your excellency has only to order up fresh cartridges.' But Oquendo stood alone, and a council of war resolved to retreat to Spain by the one course open to them, that of a circuit round the Orkneys."*

*Green's S. History of the English People, p. 421.

CHAPTER XVII.

THE SHATTERED ARMADA ESCAPING BY THE NORTH SEA.

Why did the English not follow up their advantages?

IT has been asked, "Why did not the English use their great advantages to completely destroy the Armada?" The answer is easily gathered from what we have already related. The few sentences following, written by Sir William Monson about that time, gives a true and sufficient explanation. Says he:

"The opportunity was lost, not through the negligence or backwardness of the lord admiral, but merely through the want of provivence in those who had charge of furnishing and providing for the fleet; for, at that time of so great advantage, when they came to *Because their powder and shot was spent.* examine their provisions, they found a general scarcity of powder and shot, for want of which they were forced to return."

The English fleet does grand and noble service.

It must be admitted that the English fleet did grand service. It had, during two weeks of almost continuous fighting, crippled and driven from the English shores the mightiest armament which had ever approached them—a fleet more than twice the tonnage of their own, having of all classes twice as many men, and

The defeated Armada far more costly and larger than the English fleet.

provided at a cost a hundred times greater than their own. It had also left the great Duke of Parma helpless on his transports in the canal of Ghent and Bruges, and the harbours of Newport and Dunkirk.

In that short time it had brought to ruin the plans and preparations of several years, had turned the vaunted honours and glory of confidently expected conquest into the gall and wormwood of disappointment. At the same time, we must remember and admit, that it was not all achieved by the gallant fleet of English

The arm of the unseen but Almighty Ruler of the world stretched out.

braves. There was an unseen, a Divine arm stretched out directing and overruling all—the arm of the Supreme Ruler of the world. He commanded, and this huge and diabolical scheme of wanton Spanish wrong completely failed. This fact and the mode of its accomplishment are aptly expressed in the following inscription on a medal soon after cast: *Flavit Jehovah et dessipati sunt.* The Lord blew upon them and they were scattered. This man of war, as He is called in Scripture, did by the breath of His mouth what the great sea-captains —Drake and Seymour, Hawkins and Winter, Frobisher and Howard, and all the rest—could not have done. By His winds He began, and by them as His ministers He completed, the destruction of the Armada, boastfully called invincible at the setting out. By His winds several of its great ships were lost on the seas between Lisbon and Corunna, and many injured. Again, half a dozen or more were captured or destroyed in coming up the English Channel. A full score, small and great, were destroyed or quite disabled off Calais and Gravelines. And though three-fourths of the Armada escaped, many of them hopelessly crippled from the fatal battle of Gravelines, it was only to await a more terrible destruction. On leaving the action, many of the ships were so riddled and broken, so utterly unseaworthy, that it would have been better had they been totally destroyed.

As the Armada drifted off on the evening of

Side notes:
- The mode and fact of the Lord's interposition presented in the inscription of a medal of the time.
- The winds play a chief part in the destruction of the Armada.
- Ships badly crippled and unseaworthy.

The English followed close to the Armada. the 29th from the place of action, Drake, Seymour, Howard and the rest, with all their fleet, followed. For some time they closely pursued them. The Armada, however, had neither heart nor power to renew the strife. The following sentences, from the pen of a contemporary already referred to, comprehensively describe, in his own peculiar style, the results of the contest:

"The Spaniards, that day, sustained great loss and damage, having many of their shippes shot throw and throw, and they discharged likewise great stors of ordnance againste the English; who, indeed, sustained some hindrance, but not comparable to the Spaniards' loss; for they lost not any one ship or person of account for very diligent inquisition being made, the English men all that time wherin the Spanish navey sayled upon their seas, are not found to have wanted above one hundred of their people: albeit Sir Francis Drake's ship was pierced with shot above forty times, and his very cabben was twice shot throw, and about the conclusion of the fight the bed of a certaine gentleman lying weary thereupon, was taken quite from under him with the force of a bullet. Likewise as the Earle of Northumberland and Sir Charles Blount were at dinner upon a time, the bullet of a demi-culverin broke throw the middest of their cabben, touched their feet and strooke downe two of the standers by, with many such accidents befalling the English shippes, which it were tedious to rehearse."

Fears at first that the Armada might seek shelter in Scotland but it did not.

As the Armada reached the coast of Scotland, fears were entertained that it might find allies and shelter from the Catholic lords— Huntley, Maxwell and others. It, however, passed, without entering, the Frith of Forth; and as there was no other port in the North of Scotland, which it was believed it would enter, and as their own provisions would not last longer than to return, the English fleet ceased further pursuit, but despatched two pinnaces to watch the course of the Armada. For Drake was of opinion it was making for the Cattegat in Denmark to refit, and would return in good repair during the autumn.

Drake's opinion of the Armada's destination.

As the Spanish advanced in the North Sea they found their ships were disabled.

The Spanish, it was found, had been reduced at the close of these few days of hard struggle in the English Channel, from one hundred and sixty to one hundred and ten sail.

But the winds were to work a yet greater

destruction in the still formidable, if no longer invincible Armada. When the English ceased further pursuit, the Spanish began to cast overboard all their horses and mules, in order to save water, as they said, for the soldiers; but possibly they did it because these munitions were cumbrous, and even useless, since the purpose of fighting by land had been abandoned. Many of the ships were also found to be unsafe, their hulls being so badly penetrated with shot that they were open as a sieve, very many had also lost their sails, masts, cordage and anchors, several sunk in the North Sea and perished from the fleet. Some were cast on the north coasts of Scotland, and some also on those of Norway. But few were really fit for sea. The admiral ordered all, on reaching the Orkneys, to direct their course to the coasts of Spain and Portugal, by the great Atlantic Ocean; each squadron to seek its own harbour under its own commanders.

They threw overboard the horses and mules.

Their sails, masts, cordage, helms, etc., lost.

On the 10th of August a storm more violent than any they had yet experienced overtook them and scattered their fleet. Some of them were driven on the shores of the Orkneys, others into the fiords of Norway, and were

Storms in the Northern Isles and west of Ireland.

Great loss of life. broken on the rocks, many of the seamen being drowned. The storm continued for many days longer, and drove scores of those which had hitherto escaped on the rocky coasts of the west of Ireland.

The pilot of "Our Lady of the Rosary's" report. The pilot of the Genoese ship, "Our Lady of the Rosary," on board of which was the Prince of Asculi, natural son of King Philip, thus describes her total wreck in Blasket Sound:—

"This ship was shot through four times, one of the shots was below the water mark, whereof they thought she would have sunk, and most of her tackle was spoiled with shot. Afterwards she struck on the Bleskies, a league and a half from land, upon Tuesday last at noon, and all in the ship perished, saving this examinant, who saved himself on two or three planks that were loose."

The final catastrophe of the Armada on the western coast of Ireland. The final catastrophe of the Armada came upon it in the land of its most fervid co-religionists, on the western coast of Ireland—Kerry, Galway, Mayo and Donegal. From the 10th of August to the 10th of September the Armada had been dreadfully tossed and broken among the islands and on the coasts of the North Sea. One ship after another, with

Many galleons and some smaller ships driven on Galway, Kerry and Mayo.

hundreds of those on board, had perished. The worst fell on it on the 10th of September; and later, along the line of rocky coast stretching westward, from Sligo to Eris Head, Spanish ships were seen all along the coast—two galleons put in at Dingle, seven at Garrigafoyle, several at Clew, seven in the mouth of the Shannon. The natives were terrified, and greatly exaggerate these numbers. The shipwrecked men were emaciated and spent. In every case they begged for water, from the scarcity of which they had suffered terribly. But even this was reluctantly given to the unfortunates whether they fell into the hands of the government officials, or the needy inhabitants, who were looking for the spoils, rather than to relieve the fugitives.

The great majority of the shipwrecks occurred along the bold rocky coast running in a westerly direction for full seventy miles from Sligo.

Six galleons wrecked on the cliffs of Clare.

In the same tempest in which "Our Lady of the Rosary" went down in Blasket Sound on the 10th September, six galleons were dashed with terrible violence and broken to pieces on the cliffs of Clare. Only one hundred and fifty persons succeeded in struggling through the surf to the shore All the others perished in the sea. These escaped the fury of the sea to meet a more cruel fate at Galway, a few days later. Several large ships were thrown on the Connemara coast at the same time. Most of the men escaped from the wreck to the shore. These and many others, who like them considered themselves safe on reaching land, were by order of Sir Richard Bingham, Governor of Connaught, brought to Galway, and though exhausted and powerless, were all shortly after dispatched, as enemies in arms. It was thought that though food, rest and care would have restored them, yet it was deemed dangerous so to keep them, even as the nourishing of a viper may preserve it to again bite the bosom that nourished it. There were, besides, no facilities—hospitals or provisions for sustaining such large numbers for any length of time. The religious element among the officials believed that God had given these enemies of their country and of her religion into their hands that they might destroy them. Hence their severity. That this course, foreign as it is to our ideas of

Severa dashed on the coast of Connemara.

No quarter given the Spanish, who were regarded as enemies in arms.

humanity, was not more severe than the Spanish were ready to exact on the English should they fall into their hands, is made clear from letters written about that time, when false rumours reached Paris and Madrid, assuring Philip of a grand victory. Edmund Palmer, an English merchant at San Sebastian, in Spain, wrote when this news came:—" The town made great feasts all that day, running through the streets on horseback, with rich apparel and vizards on their faces, crying with loud voices, 'That great dog, Francis Drake, is prisoner, with chains and fetters.' They also kept up dances in the night reviling her Majesty with villainous words, and when they could not do any more, with stones they broke down the windows of my house."

The Spaniards prepared to inflict cruelties on the English.

The native Irish were full of terror. They had favoured and sympathized with the Spanish cause when it seemed sure of success; but now that it had failed, they refuse to incur further danger by helping the fugitives. It was then in accord with the popular feeling, as well as by authority of the English officers, that no quarter should be given to the Spaniards. Mr. George Bingham, son of Sir Richard,

The native Irish terrified.

carried out a similar course toward the fugitives in Mayo as his father had done in Galway. In the following lines, written to his father at that time, we have an explanation of his course. Says he: "Having despatched all in both town and country, we rested Sunday all day, giving praise and thanks to Almighty God for her majesty's most happy success and deliverance from her dangerous enemies."

The disasters of the chivalrous Alonzo de Leyva were many and fatal. He survived two, and perished in the third shipwreck on these fatal coasts. He was destined to share in the doom which had fallen on the whole Armada. His brave ship the "Rata" was stranded at Bally-croy. He embarked on another galleon, which was broken on the rocks of Killibeg. In both shipwrecks he not only saved his own life, but the lives of the large company of young Spanish cavaliers, who, regarding him as the soul of Castilian chivalry, craved to be his followers. Early in October he sailed again with this gallant company on the "Gerona" from Killibeg. They crept safely along the coast, passing Tory Island and Lough Swilly, and had reached, as they thought, the

[Sidenote: through sympathizing with the religious convictions of the Spanish, now that they are vanquished, they do not wish to incur peril.]

[Sidenote: The sad end of Alonzo de Leyva and two hundred and sixty-five young hidalgos.]

open sea, when doom arrested them, and sealed their fate in a watery grave. The ship struck an unseen rock off Dunluce, and was wrecked. De Leyva and two hundred and sixty-five young Spanish hidalgos perished in this closing catastrophe of the Invincible Armada.

This the closing catastrophe of the ill-fated Armada.

The Spanish losses have been summed by a contemporary of the events as follows: Without taking into account the twenty caravels of the fleet, he says: "Of one hundred and four-and-thirty sail, which came out of Lisbon, only three-and-fifty returned to Spain. Of the four galeases of Naples, but one; the like of the largest galleons of Portugal. Of the one-and-ninety galleons and great hulks from divers provinces, only three-and-thirty returned. In a word they lost eighty-one ships in this expedition, and upwards of thirteen thousand five hundred soldiers."

Estimate of the losses by a contemporary.

There are other and more correct estimates given by other writers, who place the losses of the Spanish at a much higher figure than these. They almost all agree that the whole number of ships of all classes which returned to Spain did not exceed fifty-three, *i.e.*, about one-third of the whole number which sailed

The more accurate estimate is one hundred ships and twenty thousand men.

from Lisbon. The proportion of men who returned, there is no doubt, was about the same as the proportion of the ships, *i.e.*, one-third of the whole number which started on the expedition. Hence, as there were about thirty thousand on departing, there were about ten thousand who returned to Spain. This, we believe, is a correct estimate of the number. The following statement contains a recent and comprehensive view of the whole matter:—

"Not a single Spaniard set foot on English ground but as a prisoner; one English vessel only, and that of small size, became the prize of the invaders. The Duke of Parma did not venture to embark a man. The King of Scots, standing firm to his alliance with his illustrious kinswoman, afforded not the slightest succour to the Spanish ships, which the storms and the English drove in shattered plight upon his rugged coasts; while the Lord-Deputy of Ireland caused to be massacred without remorse the crews of all the vessels wrecked upon that island in their disastrous circumnavigation of Great Britain, so that not more than one-third of the vaunted Invincible Armada returned in safety to the ports of

Spain. Never in the records of history was the event of war on one side more entirely satisfactory and glorious, on the other more deeply humiliating and utterly disgraceful. Philip supported indeed the credit of his personal character by the dignified composure with which he listened to the tidings of this great disaster, but it was out of his power to throw the slightest veil over the dishonour of the Spanish arms, or repair the total and final failure of the Catholic cause he had so energetically espoused."—*Court and Times of Elizabeth, p. 385.*

Drake's brief statement of the loss to England by Spain.

Admiral Drake wrote, after the fleet had disappeared: "It must be confessed the Spaniards presented a sorry sight. Their invincible and dreadful navey, with all its great and terrible ostentation, did not, in all their sailing about England, so much as sink or take one ship, bark or pinnace or cok-boat of ours, or even burn so much as one sheep-cote on this land."

The real knowledge and completeness of the defeat of the Spanish.

For weeks after the defeat of the Armada, and the failure of the whole scheme of the invasion, England and Spain were alike without certain knowledge of the real state of the case. To the former the fate of the fleet was so little known that most people thought it would soon reappear and renew the attack. Proof of this is afforded by the fact that the complete organization of the army did not take place till after the defeat. The queen's activity at Tilbury, and the filling up of the ranks of both her armies to their fullest, did not occur till August and September of 1588—weeks after the defeat.

Victory of England slowly ascertained.

In Spain the tidings first received were most flattering to the king. They assured him of fame and glory from his navy—that the English fleet had been vanquished and most of its ships captured or destroyed, and that Spain was in possession of the Channel, and commanded the entrance into England. These tidings were followed by others less pleasing, intimating that only a partial success had been achieved, while some unwelcome rumours affirmed the worst. Philip remained in suspense till October, when Admiral Medina Sidonia himself arrived at Santander in Spain, and landed from his broken ships, the few surviving fragments of his grand Armada. He himself soon related to his master the sad tale of his disastrous expedition. The king listened

The sad tidings of his loss received with impassiveness by the King of Spain.

in silence, and with great composure, to the pitiable story, and after a moment or two, with an impassive voice, and in resignation of spirit, he said :—

<small>His words on being so informed.</small>

"God's holy will be done. I sent out my ships thinking I was a match for the power of England, but I did not pretend to fight against the elements. I thank God that it is no worse, and that I am able to place another fleet upon the sea if I so desire."

Sorrow was carried into very many of the most distinguished families of Spain by the loss of loved ones in this inglorious expedition. These families were putting on the usual outward badges of bereavement and signs of sorrow.

<small>The king forbids the bereaved to mourn.</small>

The king, on hearing of it, peremptorily forbade any such exhibition of grief, under pain of his displeasure. Then again, there were in some of the Spanish cities, persons who had all along looked on the whole enterprise with disfavour, and were now disposed to make merry at what they considered a ridiculous failure. These persons made some public demonstration of their feelings in Valladolid and Madrid. The king, on becoming aware of it was greatly displeased, and most peremp-

He forbids the merry to laugh. torily ordered all such to cease; and brought a few who were foremost in the folly to account, and ordered them to the block. Alas! said some of these sorely-ruled people, "Our king will neither allow us to weep nor laugh."

CHAPTER XVIII.

THE POLITICAL EFFECTS OF THE DEFEAT ON THE KING OF SPAIN.

Philip's defeat disables him from successfully attempting the further conquest of England.

WITH the destruction of the Armada, and failure of his great scheme of invasion, Philip's hopes of successfully accomplishing the conquest of England also perished. Not that his intolerance of spirit was broken or his desire to conquer his heretical foe had died; but that his courage and his resources were not equal to its achievement.

Among the English, however, a bold spirit of military adventure sprung up. In the year

An expedition goes out from England to sever Portugal from Spain and set up a king.

succeeding the defeat, a fleet of nearly two hundred ships, with twenty thousand volunteers, got up at private expense, sailed from England. Its ostensible object was to place Don Antonio, an illegitimate branch of the royal house of Portugal, on the throne of that kingdom. The expedition was under the command of Sir Francis Drake and Sir John Norris—the former to command the fleet, the latter the army. Many joined the expedition purely for adventure, and gave themselves up to plunder rather than carrying on war. They desolated Corunna and several other seaports of Spain. The object of the enterprise, however, was lost sight of, even seemed forgotten. The land and sea forces failed to make the proposed junction for the taking of Lisbon. Various disasters and wasting diseases conspired to bring the whole enterprise to complete failure.

The English expedition proved a failure every way. No good resulted. Spanish seaports desolated.

Still later another expedition set out from England under Admiral Drake, which scoured the West Indies, captured many Spanish galleons, and levied heavy tolls on the rich cities of the Spanish American colonies. Philip was naturally very indignant and determined by a second Armada to chastise the marauding parties. But his preparations were broken up by the bold descent of an English squadron (in 1596) upon Cadiz, where his stores were being collected and his preparations made. They plundered the city, destroyed all his military stores and some fifteen war-ships which he had provided. In the year following (*i.e.*, 1597) he actually

Philip's second Armada.

The second Armada totally broken by the storms.

fitted out his second Armada, which put to sea determined on a new effort of invading England. But violent storms struck it on the Bay of Biscay, and completely wrecked it, so that the last disaster was worse than the first. This was Philip's last attempt on England. His only hope henceforth of chastising her lay in reaching her through his alliances with France.

Parma's army melts away in autumn of 1588.

Parma's great army of invasion, lying in Flanders, was attacked and decimated by disease, so that in a few months it was reduced to a few thousand men. Its remnants found enough work in hindering the Low Countries from entirely casting off the yoke of Philip's authority.

His schemes for the suppression of Protestantism in France fail.

His designs on France were also at length completely frustrated. The Catholic League, through which he now operated with renewed vigour against the Huguenots, held out Philip's only hope of accomplishing his designs on behalf of the Church of Rome, and of securing a hold for himself on the kingdom of France. That hope was also doomed to disappointment. For after many vicissitudes of the struggle between the Catholics and Protes-

ENGLAND'S VICTORY OVER THE ARMADA. 173

Also the acquisition of the country for his own crown.

tants of France, the Protestant Prince Henry of Navarre ascended the French throne, and so dispelled Philip's hopes either of the ascendency of Romanism, or his own family in France. Thus, one by one, all his schemes of aggression and conquest in Europe failed. Even his own

He becomes bankrupt.

resources and credit failed; so that in ten years after the defeat of the Armada his exchequer was insolvent, and Philip laid upon

Died Sept. 13th, 1598.

the bed of death. He died in September, 1598. From the day of his defeat in the English Channel, his aggressive policy, as King of Spain, virtually closed. All the plans and schemes of his life, one after another, failed and came to naught.

The gray-headed monarch, disappointed with the failure of his darling scheme on England, and feeling little hope of success in the future,

Philip's resignation.

wrapt himself up the more closely in the cloak of a stolid religious resignation to a necessity from which he could not escape.

After having pondered for a few days on the failure and loss of his grand fleet, and on the disasters which also fell on his army, he determined to conform to the seemly dictates of religion, which command us, "in every thing to give thanks." He accordingly addressed letters to all his bishops, ordering them to observe a solemn thanksgiving in all their dioceses to Almighty God for sparing that portion of the invincible Armada which it had pleased Him to bring home again." Among his Spanish subjects the feeling generally prevailed that there was far more cause for lamentation than rejoicing, for penitence than for thanksgiving; for there were no families of any note in Spain which had not lost a member in the great catastrophe. The thanksgiving was observed in due form as ordered; but there were no expressions of heartfelt joy, nor sounds of genuine gladness.

Determines to observe a public thanksgiving.

Orders a solemn thanksgiving in Spain.

We may yet follow the results of the defeat and failure of Philip's great schemes, and the despotism from which they sprung forward, a little way into the subsequent history of Spain. Compare the Spain of the sixteenth with the Spain of the seventeenth century, or even with the Spain of the present century, and see the outcome of absolutism and despotism as opposed to the free and liberal system under which we live.

A comparison of the Spain of the sixteenth with the same country a hundred years later.

ENGLAND'S VICTORY OVER THE ARMADA.

Spain then supreme in power, in statesmen, soldiers and men of learning and letters.

In that century Spain, as we have already seen, held and exercised the highest political power among the nations of Europe. She was not only the foremost in arms, extent of territory, wealth and revenues, but she held an equal ascendency in regard to the number of eminent men which she possessed. She had not only the most renowned soldiers, sea-captains and statesmen, but also men of letters and of learning. At that day her people and her name inspired a feeling of something like awe among their neighbours. A Spaniard was regarded as a sort of incarnation of daring, malevolence, craftiness and power—an evil and malicious, but subtle and powerful, being.

How changed in one hundred years.

Look at Spain and those Spanish people one hundred years after the defeat of the invincible Armada! Oh! how we find the picture of their glory and greatness changed! How rapid and complete the downfall!! Decay and disintegration has not only set in, but, like a leprosy, has reached the nation's extremities, which are falling off, one after another, and the feeble yet remaining life shrinks into a poor and sickly trunk. The Netherland Provinces

The decay and disintegration of Spain.

ceased to belong to the monarchy of Spain after the death of Philip the Second. The small territory included in the kingdom of

The growth and greatness of Holland.

Holland, which Philip tried to crush and coerce by the might of his arbitrary power, has not only achieved its independence, but has risen to the rank of a leading power in Europe, whose commerce and civilization are far mightier in the East Indies than those of Spain. Portugal, which had been incorporated by Philip in the kingdom of Spain, has regained its autonomy and taken its place as a power co-ordinate in rank with its late master.

The provinces cease to be parts of the Spanish kingdom.

The political states or provinces of Artois, French Compté, have returned to their ancient political relationships; while such claims as Spain still held on her former possessions in Italy are feeble, and to her utterly unprofitable.

England's growth on the seas and in colonizing.

The English, and English colonists, held larger areas of the West Indies and North America than Spain, which claimed it in 1588 as absolutely her own, in right of the pope's gift and title. The power of Spain, we may add, has long since disappeared from the western world, save in the one island of Cuba.

Moreover, the army of Spain, which had been the terror of Europe under Alva, Don John, and Farnese, had become a mere handful of ill-fed, ill-paid, and ill-disciplined men.

Spain's naval and military glory pass away. The navy which, in the days of Santa Crux, De Leyva, and Oquendo, was mistress of the sea and the terror of the world, has sunk to less than one-tenth of its former self. In the seventeenth century it fell as far behind England and Holland as a hundred years before it exceeded them. Then in thrift, national prosperity, law and order, the nation had sunk beneath consideration. These qualities were not to be found in the cities, nor had they taken up their abode in the fields.

The condition of the lower population wretched. The peasantry were in poverty and on the verge of starvation. Industry had no life. The merchants were broken in resources and in spirits. The few who, as governors of provinces, viceroys or chiefs, controlled the

The rulers not in sympathy with the people. revenues, were out of touch with the masses of the people, and felt bound to them by no ties of sympathy or of interest. Intrigue, squabblings, plunderings ruled even in the royal household.

Why had Spain fallen so soon and so low, while her small dependency of Holland, and her feeble, if victorious adversary, England, had risen to power? There are two reasons— one in the arbitrary and unpaternal character of its government, which never fostered industry, manufactures, culture of mind, enlightenment, or the elevation of the masses. Nine-tenths of the population of Spain in those days were no more than the slaves to the other tenth. The other reason is, that the vivifying power of the revival of the sixteenth century was by an intolerant and despotic king and high priest, with the aid of the Inquisition, banished from Spain. The people dare not breathe the wholesome air of liberty of thought, of liberty of conscience, of civil or religious liberty. They did not learn by a happy experience the power of God in their hearts and on their lives.

Marginalia: Why Spain sank so low and so fast. Two great principles of industry and liberty disregarded.

CHAPTER XIX.

JOYFUL THANKSGIVINGS IN ENGLAND.

The people, on realizing their deliverance and the greatness of the victory, are full of joy and gratitude.

WHEN the people of England and Holland became assured of and realized how great and how complete was their victory and deliverance, and saw the utter destruction of the Spanish plot of invasion, the demonstrations of joy and gratitude were unbounded and genuine. The people of all ranks and conditions, of every shade of religious belief—the rich and poor, the nobles and common people, Churchmen and Puritans—all heartily united in rendering praise to God from whom all their blessings flowed.

Eleven Spanish flags exhibited on London bridge.

Early in September eleven Spanish flags, taken by the Londoners, were hung out on London bridge as trophies of the vanquished Armada and the defeated Spaniards. The exhibition was more creditable to the people's humanity than if, like Alva, they had brought out as many heads of prisoners and exposed them to public view on that great thoroughfare.

All recognize the hand of God and willingly respond to the calls to thanksgiving.

There is abundant evidence that a deep sense of gratitude, which sought many ways of expressing itself, pervaded the people. All felt that a menacing calamity had been averted, and a wonderful deliverance had been vouchsafed them. The hand of the Almighty had been made bare on their behalf.

Several occasions of thanksgiving were observed in the capital of the kingdom. The an-

The queen's birthday a thanksgiving holiday.

niversary of the queen's birthday, which fell on the 9th of September, was proclaimed as a general holiday and thanksgiving. Many sermons were preached and psalms sung in the churches of London. Bonfires, illuminations etc., brightened the mild autumn night following that day. Also great festivity and much rejoicing abounded in many a happy home.

The royal proclamation for a general day of thanksgiving.

The 24th of November was set apart by royal proclamation for a public and general thanksgiving throughout England. The people willingly responded to the call, and assembled in their churches, cathedrals and houses of worship to render, with united hearts and voices, thanks and praise to the Lord their God for the glorious victory and the marvellous deliverance. The whole nation united that day in singing a loud *Te Deum*, from Cornwall to Northumberland, from Kent to the shores of Wales. As on Sabbath, July the 28th, all the churches and people had humbly supplicated the Almighty for deliverance from the insolent and powerful adversary who was concentrating his forces against them at Calais and on the Flemish coast, so they now as earnestly render praise for the answer given to their prayers.

The Te Deum sung all over the land.

The thanksgiving in the cathedral of St. Paul's, London, surpassed in joyfulness, enthusiasm and splendour any in the memory of those then living. Everything looked festive at her majesty's palace of Whitehall that morning. The queen put on her most elegant royal attire. She entered her sumptuous chariot, whose seat was in the form of a throne, and which had four pillars supporting a rich canopy, and was drawn by four white horses. She was attended by her nobles and great officers, all moving in imposing grandeur to the cathedral. The queen, who ever loved splendid pageantries and shows, outshone herself in great magnificence and royal grace. All

The cathedral of St. Paul's the scene of thanksgiving.

A grand and pompous progress from Whitehall to St. Paul's.

The queen in a chariot of state, attended by her nobles and officers of state.

the line of progress was thronged with gladsome and loyal thousands, who feared God and honoured their queen. The streets through which the procession passed were hung with blue cloth, in honour of the navy. All the great London companies and guilds in goodly order lined each side of the streets along which the queen passed. Many trophies of the great victory were borne in triumphant procession. All the great sea-captains of the land whose heroism had won them renown, and England safety and glory, surrounded the queen. She graciously saluted them all, naming each one by his name. The queen bestowed a pension of considerable value on the Lord Admiral, Howard. She promised small annuities to certain of the wounded sailors, and of the more necessitous officers. On all the rest she poured gracious smiles and courteous words, which she meant to be in lieu of more substantial rewards.

Only one of the leaders of the people, who had taken active part in resisting the invasion, was wanting. The place of the Earl of Leicester, the commander-in-chief of the queen's army, long the queen's special favourite, and

The streets of London hung with blue cloth, etc.

All the great men of England.

The queen's rewards.

The Earl of Leicester had died on the 4th of Sept. inst.

ENGLAND'S VICTORY OVER THE ARMADA. 183

dear to her to the last, was empty. Returning from Whitehall to his Castle of Kenilworth, he had fallen ill on the way at Cornbury in Oxfordshire, and there, on the fourth of September, just three weeks before this thanksgiving, suddenly died. The venerable cathedral was filled with eager crowds. Thousands could not gain admission, though thousands were within its portals. The high-spirited maiden queen, her lion-hearted sea-captains, great commanders, wise statesmen, and chief nobles, bowed their heads and united their hearts with the brave sailors, gallant soldiers, and patriotic people of the land in rendering grateful and gladsome thanksgiving to the Divine Majesty who had so graciously and so marvellously wrought the nation's deliverance. The sacred walls of the venerable cathedral re-echoed that day with true expressions of the nation's gratitude and joy as the notes of the *Te Deum* rolled through its fretted aisles. With this appropriate tribute to the name of the Lord of Hosts, the grand drama of England's triumph over her Spanish invaders closed, and the curtain fell. The despot of Spain and the high priest of

Marginalia:
- The queen honours the heroes.
- All united in worship and praise to God.
- A true and loyal thanksgiving in St. Paul's Cathedral.

The King of Spain and the Pope of Rome excluded from England forever.

Rome were excluded forever from supremacy in England.* We may apply to Spain those words of Holy Writ, spoken of the invading bands of the Syrians when defeated by the King of Israel in the days of Elisha: "So the bands of Spain came no more into the land of England."

From following the historical course of events leading up to and culminating in victory, and from the becoming thanksgiving rendered to the Almighty, who bestowed it, we shall now turn to consider the character and effects, the fruits and influences, which have flowed from the victory to the parties engaged

The results and fruits of the victory to be considered in next Chaps.

---

* Elizabeth reigned almost fifteen years after the overthrow of the Armada and the defeat of the Spanish invasion. She died at Richmond on the 23rd of March, 1603, at the age of seventy, having reigned forty-five years. During these years the condition of the people, the power and influence of the kingdom, had advanced to a high elevation. Wealth had immensely increased. The national revenue, though comparatively small, had advanced a hundred per cent. The people had become united, free, independent and patriotic. Intellectual life had been thoroughly awakened, and literary men of the highest order poured forth copious and noble streams of wholesome literature. She had wrested from Spain the supremacy of the seas, and had herself become mistress of them. Her ships traversed every sea, and she led, if she did not control, the commerce of the East and West Indies.

in the conflict, especially to those descended from the victors, to the cause of human freedom, rights and progress. The struggle of 1588 also teaches lessons which we should learn and remember, and by which our attitude and conduct should be influenced. We should, as the natural and political descendants of those fathers who then struggled and secured the triumph of great and precious principles which are ever assailed yet immortal, strive to preserve and maintain them. These topics I propose considering in the chapters which follow.

CHAPTER XX.

THE CHARACTER OF THE VICTORY.

Wherein lies the greatness of a victory?

AN eye-witness, judging of a victory as complete or indecisive, grand or unimportant, would form his estimate from the qualities appearing in the parties engaged in the conflict. If the victor, though inferior in numbers and strength, by his courage, skill, impetuosity, or strategy, has overcome and driven his adversary from the field, judging from these high qualities he would pronounce it complete or grand. Nevertheless, the greatness of the victory may lie less in the character of the action, than in the cause and principles which underlie it and the fruits and effects which follow. A great poet has said with general approval,

In the cause, principles and consequences rather than the action which achieves it.

> " 'Tis the cause makes all,
> Degrades, or hallows courage in its fall."

The victory of the little band of Athenians at Marathon over a veteran army of Persians, five or six times as large, was great, even in the action. But the consequences of that victory quite eclipsed the grandeur of the action, and made it memorable for all time. For it aroused in the Athenians consciousness of power, disposed them to call it into exercise, and was the first step in their subsequent greatness. Its beneficent influence extended beyond the Athenian State to every part of Ancient Greece, and to the utmost limits of Europe. It was a check on, and a protest against despotism and barbarism, and an inspiration and impulse to freedom and civilization.

The far-reaching influence of the victory on the Athenians.

Or, when two centuries later, Scipio vanquished Hannibal and his Carthagenians at Zama, the greatness of his victory lay less in the grandeur of the action in which it was won, than in the results and consequences of the power of Rome which followed. For Hannibal in an action at Cannæ, fourteen years before, with half as many troops as his adversary, had won a more brilliant victory over the legions of Rome. But Zama was the close of Rome's struggle with the power of Hannibal and

Scipio's victory over Hannibal and the Carthagenians.

Carthage. Then the Punic wars ended. From that hour Rome's greatness, which till then trembled in the balance, became consolidated and spread, for good or evil, to the ends of the earth.

England's victory great in its achievement. The victory of England was indeed great in the noble struggle by which it was achieved. The courage, strategy, daring and impetuosity of her seamen may be paralleled, but not excelled, in the records of history. To vanquish a navy so renowned, a power so vast, as that of Spain, was glory indeed for a fleet so small, and a power so little known, as at that time England was. **Greater in its happy effects on her national life.** But the grandeur of the victory lies less in the grandeur of the action, than in its protest against intolerance and despotism; its assertion of the principles of liberty and independence for Protestantism, for the age, and for mankind. It gave a new impulse to England's national life, a foretaste and promise of her coming greatness. It constituted her the leader and patron of western civilization. Above all, it secured to her and her people the inherent and individual rights, the civil, religious, social and spiritual freedom, for which she contended.

In the words of another, we may add—"By this signal discomfiture of its most dreaded and detested foe the victory of the English nation was hailed as the victory of Protestant principles no less than of national independence; and the tidings of the national deliverance were welcomed by all the reformed churches of Europe with an ardour of joy and thankfulness proportioned to the intenseness of anxiety with which they had watched the event of a conflict, where their own dearest interests were staked along with the existence of their best ally and their firmest protector." *

<small>What part or inheritance have we in the conquests of those bygone days?</small> We may now ask ourselves, What share or inheritance in those great conquests can we claim whose lot has fallen on this western side of the Atlantic? We answer, We have all that ancestral bounty can bestow, or lawful heirship claim. We have all that rich and free heritage which they won. Let us not, then, in our earnest pursuit of material interests and personal advantage, forget this, that a legacy of moral, social and religious freedom and privilege has been bequeathed us.

---

*Aikens' Times of Elizabeth.

We may glory in conquests over the rough wastes of primeval forest, which we have reclaimed to productiveness. We may boast of those triumphs of energy and skill which have constructed great highways and waterways of travel and traffic over great stretches of land, and over lakes and rivers. We may, also, in our progress in commercial enterprise and the arts of life. But most of our conquests are on the lines and in the interests of material prosperity and civilization. Even the wars waged by the descendants of the heroes of 1588, on this side the ocean, have for the most part looked to achieving material prosperity, rather than the triumph of great economic or religious principles, or to widening the sphere of human happiness, the reign of righteousness and good-will among men.

Most of our conquests are on the lines of material prosperity.

The struggle under review is noble and instructive in these aspects of it. Those fathers struggled against despotism and for liberty, against intolerance and for freedom, against the supreme authority of man over the conscience, and for the absolute authority of God alone; against dogma, and for the rights of reason against the reign of ignorance, and for

The disparity of the two forces in numbers and resources.

the spread of knowledge. The forces which assailed them were the massed powers of the Most Catholic King of Spain, His Holiness the Pope of Rome, the Catholic League of France, and the sympathy of the whole papal world. This immensely superior force, with all its vast resources, appealing to the arbitrament of war, moved for the conquest of England and the establishment of absolute power.

<small>*This shows greatly in favour of England.*</small>

England had not then more than four and a quarter million of souls—even at the close of Elizabeth's reign she had scarcely four and a half millions. In round numbers, then, we may say she had one-tenth the population and one-twentieth the wealth, with none of the prestige of Spain. Her only ally, the little State of Holland, had not then more than a million and a half of population, and was herself engaged in a life-and-death struggle with the same enemy, on behalf of the same great principles of freedom. We must farther observe, that scarcely one-half the people of England were then Protestants, while the other half were Roman Catholics, and, therefore, in sympathy with Spain. Hence, the victory won under such circumstances has rare grandeur and a seldom equalled glory.

<small>*The disparity of the powers contending.*</small>

<small>*The Catholic population of England large as the Protestant.*</small>

The victory noble and glorious.

The inspiration under which the people and their leaders acted was not the hope of material advantage, gain or glory; but to secure freedom, independence and the exercise of their civil and religious rights.

Had Spain triumphed, how changed the life of England.

Had Spain been victorious in the Channel, had she triumphed at Gravelines, not only would freedom and national independence have fled from England, but the rights of conscience and the liberties of the age been driven into exile for many a year. The gloomiest despot, the most intolerant bigot, the most despicable man whose lot has been to rule, would have swayed the sceptre and worn the crown of the land of the free. The chief priest of Rome, and his legions of Jesuits, with the help of the Inquisition, would have turned merry England into a land of sorrow and groans, of crowded prisons and hideous scaffolds, of bloody blocks and smoking stakes.

The far-reaching fruits and results of the victory of 1588.

But the greatness of the victory reaches forward and outward beyond that land and time. It must be followed in the ever-increasing number of free and enlightened colonies, states and nations springing from that fruitful source. England was then beginning her remarkable career as a mother of colonies. She had even then made her first experiments. She had explored the Roanoke, and attempted planting that fruitful colonial vine, which she named *Virginia*, in honour of her maiden queen. A little later, a company of her conscience-respecting children colonized the regions now known as Massachusetts and Connecticut. By-and-by her colonies multiplied in number and power, and at length formed a great nationality of their own, working out a destiny for themselves—a destiny which will be grand and enduring while she adheres to and preserves the great principles which triumphed in 1588.

Settling in the colonies now forming the United States of America.

Canada, a younger daughter of the same nursing mother, includes a group of colonies, most of whom cherish the traditions, love the history, and wish to carry out the principles of government, of religion, of progress, of justice and civilization, which she inherits with the goodly dower of more than a zone of this broad continent of North America.

The Canadian colonies.

The Mother Country has still other colonies and possessions on the north and south of us— in Newfoundland and the West Indies.

Others north and south of us.

At home the four and a quarter millions have grown to thirty-six. Her United Kingdom now includes Scotland, Wales and Ireland. Her colonies are found on the high places of the earth in all parts of the Eastern Hemisphere—at Gibraltar, the Cape of Good Hope, on both the east and west coasts of Africa. Her hand is on the helm of affairs in Egypt, and her power upholds the "sick man" at Constantinople. She sways her sceptre over more than two hundred and fifty millions of the followers of Buddha and Mohammed in India, and is as potent in the islands of Sumatra and Java in the East Indies, as in those of New Providence or Jamaica in the West. She has become the teacher of civilization to the nations of the world as well as the alma mater of many nations. The throne, constitution, and vast majority of the people of England in 1888 stand fast by all the benign principles of freedom and independence, whose triumphant defence was achieved in 1588 How much farther and for how much longer, Britain's career of beneficent expansion, of civilization, liberty and power will extend, we cannot tell. Her principles of right are immortal. She cannot perish while they vitalize her.

Marginalia:
- Her possessions.
- Her greatness has been from 1588.
- It is brighter and fairer than ever before.
- All has been the outcome of these 300 years.

CHAPTER XXI.

EFFECTS OF THE VICTORY ON THE CAUSE OF FREEDOM.

A new political and moral force appears and takes its place in Europe.

THE existence of a new political and moral force was established. Protestants no longer considered it doubtful whether they could sustain themselves against the organized hostility of Spain, Rome and the Holy League. The spirit of freedom, consciousness of power and conviction of their rights had so taken possession of their minds, and these forces so animated them, that the old despotisms which ruled only by force could no longer repress them. Philip's hopes now turned to and centred in the Catholic League, whose leader, supported by Philip's gold, was that unscrupulous Catholic, the Duke of Guise. Through his intermeddlings with the internal affairs of France and the influence of his money, the King of Spain now saw with joy the whole

Protestant principles and convictions cannot be repressed by force.

population of France divided into two hostile camps—the Leaguers and the Huguenots.

The year following the defeat of the Armada, Henry III. of France fell by the hand of an assassin, and Henry of Navarre, under the title of Henry IV., the leader of the Huguenots, claimed the crown of France. This heroic young prince was every inch a soldier and a king, and in the face of Philip, the League and the Guises, ascended the throne of France.

The Pope, Philip, and the League, all denounced Henry as a heretic, and aroused and incited the Catholics of France against him. He triumphed after a severe and sanguinary contest, and a Protestant prince sat upon the throne of France. Influenced by his political interests—for Henry looked on both Protestantism and Romanism only as means to an end—he renounced Protestantism and espoused Romanism, saying, "Surely France is worth a mass." But he continued to befriend his old allies; and in 1598 the famous edict of Nantes became law, securing a recognition to the Huguenots of equal civil and religious rights.

Though England had successfully asserted her protest against the supremacy of the pope, she had not affirmed the supremacy of Christ, but had transferred the headship of the church to her sovereign. He had not yet learned to practice the toleration which inheres in the principles of Protestantism. Queen Elizabeth held on this point the same opinions as her father, Henry VIII. He sent Catholics to the stake for denying his own supremacy, and Protestants for denying the Romish doctrine of Transubstantiation. She would allow no supremacy which she supposed infringed on her own. She rated with unsparing severity, or promptly punished, any one, whether in parliament, through the press, or in the pulpit, who infringed on her prerogative. She refused freedom of debate on any question which touched this tender point.

She sent persons to prison who wrote or published things offensive to her. A Mr. Penry, a Welsh minister, the supposed author of a squib entitled, "Martin Marprelate," was tried for felony. He was charged with saying, in the way of aspersion of the queen's good faith, that "the queen, having been put on her throne by the gospel, had suffered the gospel to reach no further than the end of her sceptre." For this he was found guilty, was sentenced and hanged. Another Puritan minister, Mr. Udal, was tried, condemned and thrown into prison, where he was detained till he died. The plea of conscience, for which Elizabeth had previously affirmed her respect, did not save them.

Udal imprisoned.

Elizabeth's greatest severities arose from her zeal in enforcing uniformity of worship, or conformity to the service of the Established Church. She did not punish men for their opinions or doctrines, but for refusing to conform. She hated Anabaptists, sectaries and all kinds of dissent, and punished them with imprisonment, confiscation of goods and banishment. She thus argued: "To allow churches with contrary rites and ceremonies were nothing else but to sow religion out of religion, to distract good men's minds, to cherish factious men's humours, and to mingle divine and human things."

Elizabeth punished non-conformity severely.

Hated dissent.

Queen Elizabeth's fight for uniformity.

Her Protestantism came far short of the liberal, truly catholic and comprehensive Protestantism of that most virtuous and noble representative of it in the Low Countries—William the Silent, whose assassination Philip had effected four years previous to the inva-

Her Protestantism compared with that of William the Silent, Prince of Orange.

ENGLAND'S VICTORY OVER THE ARMADA. 199

His the type of that which is now approved and accepted in all Protestant and Christian countries.

sion. His included general toleration of every form of Christian worship which men's consciences bound them to render. He desired that in the Low Countries freedom should be given Episcopalians and Puritans, Anabaptists and Catholics, Calvinists and Lutherans. He was a strict Calvinist himself, and would have secured this larger liberty for his own country had not the bullet of the assassin cut him off in the midst of his day.

Elizabeth's Protestantism was again very different in its principles from the Romanism of her adversary, Philip of Spain. He punished every form of dissent with burying, or burning alive, with drowning, imprisonment, torture or exile. Elizabeth was opposed, at least in her earlier years, to putting any one to

The Jesuits and others of the Catholic priests who suffered capital punishment, did so for treason, not for their faith.

death on account of his religious beliefs. She did not then exceed imposing fines, banishment or imprisonment. Those Jesuits, priests, and seminarian renegades who returned after having been banished, and engaged in treasonable practices, were executed, not for believing in transubstantiation or the seven sacraments, but for treason, and for teaching the people it was right to disown and murder their queen.

CHAPTER XXII.

ITS EFFECTS ON ENGLAND'S NATIONAL LIFE.

The progress of modern life incompatible with the beliefs and usages of mediæval times.

THE supremacy of the pope, the absolute power of kings, obedience to mediæval dogmas and forms of religion, were proved by the victory of 1588 to be inconsistent with national growth, independence of thought, love of liberty, and the full development of Protestantism. The results of the struggle were marvellous and manifold. Many hitherto open questions were thereby permanently settled. In the first place, the

The ascendency of Protestantism secured.

Protestant ascendency was secured, not only in England, but also in the Netherlands. In the latter country the struggle with Spain was above everything else, we may say was solely, for religious freedom—for liberty of conscience, of thought, of belief and of worship. The destruction of the Armada paralyzed the power of the Inquisition in those provinces and settled forever their severance from the crown and kingdom of Spain.

<small>It leads to the breaking up of the Catholic League.</small>
It also prepared the way for and led to the breaking up of the Catholic League, whose vital principle was death to Protestantism, to freedom of thought, belief or worship, all of which was branded as heresy. It settled the fate of the Duke of Guise, the leader of the armies of the League. It determined the stability of the Reformation in those states of Germany which had previously received it. To

<small>It leads also to the elevation of the Protestant Prince Henry of Navarre to the throne of France.</small>
it also, and to the power it exercised on the French nation, may largely be ascribed the elevation of the Protestant Prince Henry of Navarre to the throne of France. It also confirmed James VI. of Scotland in his profession of attachment to the reformed religion established in his land, and held out the strongest

<small>It confirmed James VI. in his attachment to the reformed religion.</small>
motives to induce him, as heir-presumptive to the throne of England, and successor to Queen Elizabeth, to firmly adhere to and defend the Protestant religion.

The victory of 1588 led the great majority of the Roman Catholic population of England to conform to the Protestant religion, and gathered them and those hitherto indifferent about religion, into the Church of England. Many who had hitherto hoped for a restoration of the ancient religion now saw their dream dissipated, and a wider gulf than ever separating England and Rome. A majority, perhaps, of the English people had up to that time hoped that with the advent of a new sovereign, particularly while the Queen of Scots lived, who was heir, after Elizabeth, to the crown, that the papal religion would be again established.

<small>Drew in the Catholics into the Established Church.</small>

<small>This the wisest and the safest course.</small>

The events of the year extinguished all such hopes. For even James VI. of Scotland, Mary's son, who was sure to succeed Elizabeth, having espoused the reformed religion, and having shown no signs of sympathy with Philip or the Catholic League, gave no ground for them to expect anything in that direction. There was no cheering prospect, therefore, before them. It was either conformity, or privation, hardship, suffering or persecution. For the queen, though opposed neither to Romish doctrines nor persons, rejected entirely the supremacy of the pope and asserted her own. She entertained up to this period of her life an affirmed

<small>Elizabeth not inclined to persecution before 1588.</small>

aversion to persecution for matters of conscience, and to the Inquisition in all its forms.

The queen becomes a persecutor in enforcing conformity.

But she insisted on uniformity of outward rites and worship. In her latter years she carried out her notions with a severity which no refinement of reasoning or stretch of charity can justify. In enforcing this anti-Protestant enactment she punished Catholics and Protestants, Anabaptists and Calvinists with equal severity. Indeed the evidence goes to show

More inclined to favour Catholic than Protestant nonconformists.

that she inclined more to favour Catholic nonconformists than Protestant. For in her doctrinal beliefs she was more Catholic than Protestant. Her court, during most of her life, was more than half filled by young Catholics. The Puritans had been her safety and defence, had stood by her in all emergencies, and had shown the highest rectitude, loyalty, capacity and character in her service. Her great ministers, Cecil, Walshingham, Davison and others were Calvinists. They had

The conspicuous talents and character of the Puritans about the queen.

formed and shown her how to administer every wise and great measure, which led to her greatness and success.

The Catholics, on the other hand, had conspired against her, had risen in insurrection, had plotted for taking away her life. Six of the young persons engaged in the Ballard and Babbington plot to destroy her life, were young Catholics residing in her household. These being proved guilty were, by law, executed. Her great ministers, whom we have just named, and others of like fidelity and ability, received scant rewards and small thanks from her for their splendid services. Walshingham, to whose skill and fidelity she owed the discovery and exposure of the plot, died penniless, and she even allowed his effects to be sold to pay some debt said to be due her, while his family received no pension or consideration from the queen. Notwithstanding her illiberal treatment of her Puritan supporters, no one of them was ever charged with disloyalty to her.

Six of the conspirators in the plot for the queen's life were of her own household.

Illiberal to her Puritan minister Walshingham.

The feelings of English Catholics rose to something like patriotism when they saw that Philip meant to destroy the nation's independence, and make England a province of his kingdom, or dependency for one of his children or appointees. In the failure of Philip's great enterprise, undertaken in the name of religion, and at the wish, and with the sanction of the pope, they saw a solemn appeal to

In the struggle many of the Catholics become patriotic in their feelings. They become strongly English.

ENGLAND'S VICTORY OVER THE ARMADA. 205

The superstition of the age evoked the result of the struggle as an expression of the will of Heaven against Spain, and for England.

the ordeal of war, going against the church, and in favour of the queen. The superstition of that age was so strongly in favour of that mediæval mode of settling weighty and subtle questions, that a strong revulsion of feeling set in afterward among the Catholics. The winds of heaven, the seas and tempests, were regarded as God's ministers, and the favour of Heaven had been invoked by the vicegerent of Christ, and his blessing bestowed with fullest assurance of success; yet total and terrible failure had followed.

This view prevailed generally with the Catholics.

All the circumstances and occurrences of the struggle signified the disapprobation of the God of battles to the side in whose favour their prejudices lay. There was a general acquiescence in the belief that the decision of Heaven was for England, and against Spain. No event of modern history, not even the landing of William of Orange, or the battle of Waterloo, furnishes such manifold and palpable evidence of the will of the Supreme Ruler than is shown in the failure of the Spanish invasion of England and the grand catastrophe with which it closed. The battle of Gravelines was as truly the triumph of

The battle of Gravelines as truly a triumph of liberty as the battle of the Boyne of the rights of conscience.

Protestantism and liberty over Romanism and despotism, as the battle of the Boyne under William, just one hundred years later, was the triumph of freedom of conscience over subjugation of its rights to either pope or king. If Queen Elizabeth's prestige was high before the invasion, it was much higher after. The splendid abilities, courage and patriotism of Admiral Drake, the greatest of England's sea-captains, outshone the foremost admirals of the Armada. He was not only the grandest of England's many noble naval commanders and fighters, but he was second to none in the world.

Admiral Drake the foremost naval commander of his day.

English supremacy upon the ocean followed the downfall of Spain.

The star of the British navy then rose above the national horizon. It soon displaced Spain from her supremacy upon the ocean, and became itself mistress of the seas. Through all the vicissitudes of revolution and change of dynasty, from that time till now, she has not surrendered her rule upon the wave. A sense of yet untried power, the true index of undeveloped greatness, possessed the hearts of the younger generation of both nobles and people at that time. We venture to believe that a sense of mature and unspent power, greater than ever before, lies in that glory-covered arm of her power, in 1888. The question of religion soon became identified in the minds of the victors with that of country. Unhappily, as we think, the queen clung with uncompromising tenacity to her notions of uniformity. She failed to discover or learn the possibilities that lay within her power, in granting a general toleration of religious worship. It was reserved for a later time, and further outworking of the principles of Protestantism to establish it in all parts of the British realm.

> *England's power on the sea still fresh and unspent.*

> *Elizabeth's notions about uniformity blind her eyes to the blessings of toleration.*

Mr. Froude, with equal justness and truth, says, concerning the influence of the great awakening of the sixteenth century: "The countries which rejected the Reformation never again had freedom offered to them in the dress of a purer religion. The rejection returned upon them as a revolution, as the negation of all religion. In Austria, in Spain, in France, in Italy, the Church has been stripped, step by step, of its wealth, of its power, even of its control over the education of the people. Practical life has become secularized, and culture and intelligence have ceased to interest themselves in a creed which they no longer believe. Doctrine may be piled upon doctrine. The laity are contemptuously indifferent, and leave the priests in possession of the field in which reasonable men have ceased to expect any good thing to grow. This is the only fruit of the Catholic reaction of the sixteenth century, of all the efforts of the Jesuits and the Inquisition, of the Council of Trent, the massacre of St. Bartholomew, and the religious wars of Philip II. . . . While the Church of Rome is losing the countries it persuaded to refuse the Reformation, it exults in the converts which it is recovering from the nations which become Protestant. It fails to see that its success is its greatest condemnation. Protestantism alone has kept alive the sentiment of piety which, when allied with weakness of intellect, is the natural prey of superstition."

CHAPTER XXIII.

EVIDENCES OF THE RULING OF A DIVINE HAND.

Bentivoglio's opinion of the rule of Divine Providence.

WE approve the following just and well-expressed judgment, by the enlightened foreigner, Mr. Bentivoglio, in reference to the catastrophe of the Armada of Spain, which threatened the overthrow of the power of England.

Says he: "Few enterprises were ever more deeply weighed, few preceded by more immense preparations, and none, perhaps, ever attended with a more unfortunate issue. How vain and fallacious are the best concerted schemes of men! Thus often Divine Providence, in the wisdom of His impenetrable designs, has determined the fate of our enterprises quite contrary to the presumptuous expectations of human foresight." *

---

* Tytler, Vol. V., p. 89.

We of eighteen eighty-eight ought to learn from fifteen eighty-eight this lasting and obvious lesson, viz., that the overruling hand of Divine Providence directed and determined the result of the contest. The same hand is indeed similarly related to all the occurrences and events of individual, national and general history. For God is in the outworking as He is the final end of the course of human events. In no great crisis of modern times is the display of a Divine control more manifestly shown than in England's victory over the Armada and the invading hosts of Spain. As the fate of Waterloo in 1815 was not entirely due, on the one hand, to the decline of Napoleon's mental powers, the weakness of his army, or the slipperiness of the battle-ground from recent rains; so neither was it, on the other, to a special exaltation of Wellington's genius, the greater bravery of the allied armies, or their more advantageous position or movements; but because the will of the Supreme Ruler directed and controlled the issues of the day. This was most impressively so in England's struggle with the Spanish Armada in the English Channel in 1588. God's presiding

[sidenotes:]
A most obvious lesson, *i.e.*, that God's hand directed and determined the result.

The hand of God presiding and His will determining at Waterloo.

The control and direction of Providence manifest in the Channel struggle of 1588.

presence was as manifest in the incidents and occurrences of that momentous crisis, and as impressively felt in the history of the Anglo-Saxon race, as His presiding presence was impressively stamped upon the history of the children of Israel at the Red Sea and by the Jordan. The facts of the case should be remembered, and their obvious significance admitted, otherwise we will not learn the lessons they teach. Observe this, then,

<small>In the death of the Capt.-General of the Armada, causing a delay of a month.</small> from the first, that when the Captain-General of the Armada, that able and experienced sea-captain, the Marquis of Santa Crux, had his fleet ready to sail from Lisbon, he was taken seriously ill and suddenly died. The vice-admiral also, who was little less honoured for his naval skill, unexpectedly died about the same time. This caused a delay of a month in the sailing of the Armada. Philip and Parma <small>This gave the English a little time to prepare to resist them.</small> had successfully deceived Queen Elizabeth with their protracted peace negotiations, so that she did not make, but even hindered preparations from being made, to resist the Armada, till the last moment. This month was of great value in England, in affording so much more time to get into some measure of readiness.

The death of the great admiral was profitable to the English in another way, viz., that it gave them less ability and experience with which to cope when the crisis came.

The violent storm off the coast of Spain caused a delay of a month at Corunna to refit.

Again, after the Armada had put to sea, the violent storm which scattered the ships, sinking some, disabling others, and in some measure injuring all, caused a further delay of a month in refitting at Corunna. This again afforded the English longer time for preparing and strengthening their still comparatively small navy. Also, the mistake of Admiral Medina,

Mistaking the Lizard for the Plymouth light.

in making for the Lizard rather than the Plymouth light, gave opportunity to the pirate Fleming to inform Admiral Howard of the enemy's approach, and afforded him time to get his fleet safely out of Plymouth harbour, before his adversary had opportunity to capture or destroy his navy, as he intended. Had the Armada proceeded to England without any of these delays, she would have found her

England not prepared to resist till last moment.

unprepared, and might have made a successful landing upon her shores. But the delays lost great opportunities to Spain, and opened new and brighter ones to England. Moreover, the winds were favourable for collecting and mov-

ENGLAND'S VICTORY OVER THE ARMADA. 213

English acquire confidence from opening success.

ing the light English ships through all their way up the Channel, so that in the opening engagements they were able to get the weather-gage, and so acquire confidence in their ability to deal with their great adversary.

On the memorable Sabbath night of July the 28th, the wind, the tide, even the darkness, favoured the successful issue of the strategical effort to throw the Spanish fleet into panic and confusion. This seemingly small matter in so great a struggle enabled Drake and Seymour, Hawkins and the rest, to enter on the memorable and crowning struggle of the 29th of July, off Gravelines. The English cannon, which did such splendid service that day, did not alone, however, achieve the glorious results of the day. If the stars in their courses fought against Sisera, so did the winds against the invincible Armada. They blew the Spanish ships up the Channel, close on the Flemish shallows, drove them into clusters too close, one to another, for efficient action. They also rendered return to Calais impossible—a move the admiral designed to make that morning, but was hindered as well by the winds as the English guns. Yet the armament was still very strong in numbers of men and ships at the close of the action of the 29th. Though not less than twenty to thirty of its ships and five or six thousand of its men had melted away since entering the Channel, it still had from a hundred and ten to a hundred and twenty ships, even if many of them were crippled and nearly broken.

The number of their men was still vastly more than those of the English, even if they were beaten and disheartened. Had the winds abated, or had they become favourable, the English expected that they would return in a few days, and might successfully form a junction with Parma off the French coast, and guard his army to their shores. The winds proved themselves powerful allies to England, so that they became light and deliverance to her, and darkness and destruction to the Armada. God blowed upon them and they were scattered. By far the greater part of the Armada's destruction was accomplished by them. Increasing in fury, the storm drove them along the north coasts of Scotland, past the Orkneys, some of them still farther north; and then, with a violence of winds and waves seldom paralleled, dashed them on the rough and rocky western shores of Ireland—Kerry, Galway, and Donegal, and some of them on the no less fatal shores of the isles of Mull and Arran. The destruction in these ports was terrible and fatally complete, for not less than two score galleons and ten thousand men perished on those wild coasts among their Irish co-religionists.

The destruction of the Armada completed on the west of Ireland and western isles.

This all but total destruction of the Invincible Armada, and with it the failure of the whole scheme of invasion, bears the mark of the Divine Hand. When it became fully known in England the impression produced on the minds of all Catholics, quite as much as Protestants, was deep and enduring; for all knew that the King of Spain and the Holy Father at Rome had appealed in the defence of their cause to the ordeal of war, and looked for the arbitrament of Heaven, through it to settle the strife. The winds and seas were regarded as especially God's ministers. The result was open and decisive. England was, by the test, declared in the right; Spain and the Church of Rome in the wrong.

The impression made on English Catholics by the providential decision of the strife deep and enduring.

It was for freedom against intolerance, for Protestantism against Romanism. The results profoundly impressed the English Catholics, and did much to decide them to conformity to the established religion. Considerations of utility and the hopelessness of any early or easy change of the national religion also had their influence.

CHAPTER XXIV.

OUR HERITAGE SHOULD BE PRESERVED.

The heritage fallen to us demands watchfulness.

BUT this is not all. Fifteen hundred and eighty-eight recalls the cost and suggests the value of the heritage of freedom — social, intellectual and religious, which has fallen to us. It also calls us to the exercise of perpetual vigilance and earnest endeavour to preserve and transmit the same to those who follow.

The unreformed countries and peoples have fallen behind in progress.

Those nations—Spain, France, Italy, and the rest—which in the sixteenth century excluded the Reformation, with its beneficent and quickening influences, have fallen behind in the march of progress. Statistics show the continued reign of illiteracy among the masses,

The reformed have advanced.

and corresponding lack of enterprise and independence; while England, Germany, the United States, and all those peoples who heartily received it, or have sprung from

The masses enlightened. those who did, have steadily advanced in prosperity and enlightenment, and now lead the van of civilization. It is not easy to measure, nor possible to exaggerate the elevation, the power and true manliness of character which it imparted to those communities, peoples and nations which received it; nor is it to estimate the sources of happiness and prosperity which it opened to them.

The same spirit as of old seeks to gain the mastery under new forms, names and modes. Let us be well aware that the same spirit of despotism under different forms and names, still lives in that system, which makes its proud boast that it is *semper eadem*—always the same. It wishes now, as of old, to subvert the fair fabric of our Protestantism, and snatch from mankind the liberties which have been secured at such great cost. The means now employed for this are less grim and repellant than of old.

Not now force, but persuasives. It does not now propose to convert us by the power of the sword, or the pains of the Inquisition; but by the subtilties of the Jesuit, and the persuasives of a persistent propagandism, Rome puts on the garb and speaks in the language of an angel of freedom and human rights, that so she may restore in the nineteenth century the sway of that mediævalism which she lost in the sixteenth. If she continues to denounce the Reformation, it is an admission that its principles are still a power which she dreads. In his encyclical of 1885, Leo XIII. expressed himself in such phrases as these in regard to the Reformation. He denounced it as " the origin of all the now active principles of unbridled liberty." He repudiated the notion, "that every man should be allowed freely to think on whatsoever subject he pleases." He condemned those "governments which allow every one to follow the form of religion he prefers."

The present pope's condemnation of the Reformation.

In his encyclical of the present year he expounds and defines the sphere of religion and of liberty. It is curious to observe the plausible, almost Protestant, language in which he sets forth his notions of human rights and liberties, and conceals his undying yearning for universal and absolute power. We must discriminate between his theories and practice in regard to men's religious and civil rights. For they are widely different. He conditions and limits them on all sides by his own will. As the waters surround and limit, and so define our notion of an island, so does his will surround

Criticisms of the pope's encyclical for 1888.

and limit all his theories of liberty. Whatever he may describe as the proper sphere of either religion or liberty in thought, speech or action, may be modified and must be administered according to that will. He regards the Church of Rome, of which he is the head, as the custodian of those blessings, and men and nations to enjoy just so much of them as he deems proper to dispense.

What it is, and where tolerated.

Read the following extract from his encyclical of this year, and judge what it means. He says:

Extract from his ecyclical for 1888.

"It is necessary that there should be some profession of religion in the community, and that the religion thus professed should be the true one. It is not difficult, at least in Catholic countries, to recognize by unmistakable signs which is the true religion. This religion the heads of the State are bound to protect and to maintain, in the true interests of the community. For the powers that be are established for the benefit of those governed; and though the immediate end of the State is to secure the welfare of the citizens in the present life, it is also in duty bound not to diminish, but to foster in man that faculty of attaining to the supreme good, in which lies his everlasting blessedness, and this attainment is impossible without religion."

These are not wild or extravagant, but plausible and measured words. Still it is clear enough what the pope means by "the true religion." He means simply that of the Romish Church, of which he claims to be the infallible head, whether that church be organized in England, Canada or the United States. If the head of the State is bound to protect it, as he claims it should, then are civil rulers bound to use their power to maintain one as against another form of religion. Hence the course of Philip the Second and Sixtus the Fifth, may be rightly followed by other princes. Hence, also, all false religions, *i.e.*, all except the papal, being in the opinion of that not impartial judge, pestilential and damning, should now, as of old, be suppressed. Then, if the state is in harmony with the church, it should acknowledge the church's right to require obedience from all the people to her dictates, and it is the state's duty to enforce, by means of her power, such obedience. All history reminds us how that whenever the state accepted Rome's teachings as to her sphere and duty, human freedom became impossible. If the state should now carry out the church's will and support

Side notes:
His notions about "true religion."
How it tolerates.
How it refuses toleration.
How he determines the religion the state should support.
All history teaches us that if the state accepts Rome's teachings as to her duty, liberty is impossible.

what she defines "true religion," then all forms of religion, however beneficent, pure and true, which differ from that religion, would in no wise be longer tolerated. When, again, the church and state are not in harmony, *i.e.*, when the state is on the side of freedom, the pope would then agree to a system of religious toleration, which would secure his form of religion on equal toleration with the one with which the state is in harmony. But when the state is in harmony with the Church of Rome, he promises no such equal toleration to the other party. This is equal to saying, Where the state is papal, the papal religion, and no other should be tolerated; but when the state is Protestant, there equal religious toleration should be granted to the papal as well as to the Protestant.

Liberty bound up with Protestantism. Hence it follows that liberty which has been bound up with Protestantism for three-and-a-half centuries, is tolerated only in states not in harmony with Rome; but in states in agreement with her or such as come into agreement with her theories and doctrines, toleration gives way to papal supremacy and to the rule of absolute power.

It surely becomes those who inherit, as we do, the great boon of Christian freedom, to remember how these blessings have been won, and at how great a cost; and so vigilantly preserve and defend them against the persistent and insidious attacks of Rome.

Our duty to preserve the boon we inherit.

In the present day, one of the boasts of Romish propagandists is that they are making rapid progress in reconverting those peoples who, in the sixteenth century, renounced the pope's supremacy and filled up the ranks of the Reformation. Especially is this boast often made of the Anglo-Saxon race and people. If this is true, though we do not believe it is, it would be remarkable, that while all those countries which rejected the Reformation and clung to mediævalism have fallen behind in the march of civilization, and the Romish Church has lost her power over them, that the Anglo-Saxon race, which has experienced beyond others the vivifying and beneficent influence of the Reformation, has passed into and leads the van of progress, should now yield to priestcraft and enter the ranks of reaction. If this view is correct, then one or the other of these inferences follows: First, that Rome has so stultified

The boast of Romanists that they are recovering the reformed countries.

All unreformed countries have fallen behind the reformed in the march of progress.

The Romish boast not creditable to the vitality and power of their religion.

and deadened spiritual life in those who clung to her that she no longer has the moral and spiritual forces necessary to bind them to her and assure them she can do them any good; or, second, it goes to show how vital and how powerful for good Protestantism has been since out of the exuberance of its life it is able to impart vitality and vigour to the effete and decadent system of Rome. Certainly such perversion of Protestants argues little in favour of the spiritual power of the Romish system, while it compliments the vitality and spiritual power of Protestantism.

The boasters mostly perverts expressing their desires.

It will be found, we believe, that those who boast most loudly of the success of their efforts, not to convert men to the faith that is in Jesus, but to pervert them to the faith of the pope, are themselves perverts; and the Jesuitical modes employed by them are as little defensible or honourable, as evangelical or spiritually profitable. We may even regard it true, that the words which express their success are rather expressions of the desires and hopes of those who use them, than of actual results. That great efforts are, however, being made, some success attending them, and high hopes of future triumph are entertained, is evident from such vivid portrayals of the work as the following: Dr. Vaughan, the Romish Bishop of Salford, England, speaking of the progress of popery in England, recently said:

<small>The statement of one of them.</small>
"A few years ago the Anglican bishops, with one or two exceptions, were shocked by the departure of the Ritualists, and the Legislature was again and again invoked to put down the Romanising tendencies. Still the practices have gone on; churches in which Ritualism is adopted are arising all over the land, under the jurisdiction of Anglican bishops, until *Catholics can scarcely distinguish between such places and the churches belonging to their own communion.*

"Even the great Cathedral of St. Paul in London is being turned to resemble more a Catholic church than anything else; a magnificent altar and reredos have been erected, which could not have been more effectively designed by an architect in Rome, so perfect are the outlines and decorations. It is now only necessary to provide the relics of the saints and secure the blessing of the Catholic Church in order to celebrate High Mass."

He then specifies the aspects of growth in many particulars during thirty or forty years now past. He states that from two or three

The growth of Romanism in England.

hundred priests the number has increased to as many thousands. From two or three score convents and schools the number has reached several hundred. The number of churches has kept full pace with the number of priests. They have now a complete hierarchical system set up, which covers the whole land, and from among clerical perverts they have found bishops, archbishops and cardinals, and all the rest.

Perverts from among the Church of England's clergy.

Perhaps the most discouraging view of the whole matter is the Romanising or ritualistic tendencies and proclivities of not a few ministering in the Church of England, who look lightly on the whole work of the Reformation in proportion to their nearness of approach to the Church of Rome. The eloquent words uttered by Mr. Disraeli in Glasgow, in 1874, in a memorable speech, may have something prophetic in them. Said he:

Mr. Disraeli

"It may be open to England again to take her stand upon the Reformation, which three hundred years ago was the source of her greatness and her glory; and it may be her proud destiny to guard civilization alike from the withering blast of atheism, and FROM THE SIMOOM OF SACERDOTAL USURPATION."

CHAPTER XXV.

A LESSON FROM THE FATHERS OF 1588 TO THEIR CANADIAN CHILDREN.

The fathers entrust us as their heirs with the care of all they won for us.

IF we are the offspring of the patriotic fathers who triumphed in 1588—as we certainly are—then are we also their heirs and successors, and should ascertain what they have left us, and how we should preserve and use it. They bestowed upon us a rich inheritance of independence, manly enterprise, free institutions, freedom of thought, of action and of religion, respect for law, the rights of fellow-men, and an open Bible. These have made our race strong, enlightened, powerful and prosperous—the foremost in the march of progress and civilization. Our ancient adversaries are also on the soil of Canada, in their representatives of the unchanging Church of Rome. They are the offspring and heirs of the principles, traditions and beliefs for which Philip the

The old adversaries are also here full of the same spirit as of old.

Second and Sixtus the Fifth contended. They encounter us under the full inspiration of the same spirit of subtlety, intolerance, lust of power, longing for the conquest of this new world for themselves. Romanism, having exhausted its power over the peoples of Italy, Austria, France, and all those countries from which, with fire and sword, she expelled Protestant liberty in the sixteenth century, she here seeks the conquest of new fields. She pours into Great Britain, Canada and the United States her Jesuit militia, her meek-faced nuns and grim-faced monks, with a full-grown hierarchy, parasite-like, to live upon, and, if possible, exhaust its free, young life. She has large and profitable investments in various corporations which yield her liberal revenues, but from all taxation she claims exemption on the ground of the spiritual benefits she affects to bestow upon the state. She legally holds in Quebec a position of strength not only superior to Protestantism, but above what she holds in any other province of the Dominion of Canada, or in any one of the United States of America, For the church in that province is established and supported by

Seeks dominance in the land.

Having lost her hold on the Catholic countries of Europe, the Church of Rome wishes to regain England, Canada, and the United States.

The Church of Rome established and supported by the state in Quebec.

Repudiates equality and practises her theory of supremacy.

Exercises a hurtful influence in politics, education, etc.

law. She repudiates the doctrine of equal rights with other bodies of Christians, and there realizes her own theory of supremacy not only over other churches, but over the state as well. In her eagerness to grasp power she aims at controlling education, politics, all public institutions such as schools, colleges, convents, hospitals and asylums. She wishes to exercise a power as great in every province of the Dominion. In the meantime she does not diffuse among the people healthful principles of independence, of inquiry, of equal rights and of liberty, but of submission and implicit obedience to ecclesiastical authority. The church's property and revenues in Quebec are quite beyond what almost any citizen in this province imagines, because he hears the cry so constantly of provincial importunity, begging for more money from the national treasury.

Her revenues derived from tithes, fees for special masses, sacraments and services, rents of properties, lotteries and such like, amount annually to from eight to ten million dollars, which would give for the expense of its nine hundred parishes, on an average, a revenue of more than eight thousand dollars a year.

The following statement, prepared with much care by the Rev. A. B. Cruchet, of Montreal, may be regarded as by no means an over-statement of the property and revenues of the Romish Church in Quebec:

"In 1759 she received 2,117,000 acres of land, which valuable possession has since been greatly added to by property gained by diplomacy and continual begging, and by the natural increase in the values of certain kinds of real estate. She owns nine hundred churches, valued at $37,000,000; nine hundred parsonages, along with the palaces of the cardinal, the archbishops and bishops, valued at $9,000,-000; twelve seminaries, worth $600,000; seventeen classical colleges, $850,000; two hundred and fifty-nine boarding-schools and academies, $6,000,000; eight hundred convents, $4,000,000; sixty-eight hospitals and asylums, $4,000,000—a total of $61,210,000. As to lands, shops, houses and invested capital, it is impossible to reach absolute certainty. We know that some ecclesiastical orders are enormously rich. Catholics themselves declare that the Sulpicians, for example, are richer than the Bank of Montreal, the most powerful institution of the kind in America."

Last year, the Jesuits, who had been suppressed in 1774, more than one hundred years ago, and have been without legal domicile in the land ever since, were incorporated with the papal approbation by the Romish province of Quebec. In the current year the Catholic premier of the province, has passed a bill to indemnify the order for its previously escheated property as a future outfit and endowment to the extent of four hundred thousand dollars. This act for the endowment of these pernicious intruders is now before the Dominion Government for approval or disallowance. If allowed, it becomes law. It remains to be seen whether the government will have the courage to disallow the measure, seeing it is entangled in the meshes of a network of political influence and intrigue from which it requires boldness to escape. There are strong and varied reasons why the measure should not be allowed to become law in Canada. In the first place, the province is unable to pay the money out of its own funds. It is already overwhelmed with a debt of twenty-two millions; and is constantly begging aid from the Dominion Government to meet its current expenses. Again, neither the

The endowment of the Jesuits should not be allowed.

Has the government of the Dominion independence to disallow the Provincial Act.

Reasons why it should be disallowed.

The province not able to pay the endowment granted.

incorporation nor endowment of the order should be allowed because no other country has given a state endowment to it. In fact, most Catholic countries have either refused the Jesuits legal domicile or forcibly expelled them. They are now prohibited from taking any part in public education in France, Belgium and Germany. Even in Italy they have no foothold, save in the city of Rome. In Austria they are under surveillance, and they are wholly excluded from Mexico. These are Catholic countries, be it observed. They were excluded many years ago from England, though they there conduct schools and colleges, not, however, at the state's, but at their own expense.

The order regarded pernicious and excluded from Catholic as well as Protestant countries in Europe.

In the third place, it is invidious to endow this brotherhood and pass over other Catholic societies, which, if there is any truth in history, are far more deserving than this one. It not only grants them equal rights with old and reputable societies, but it puts a premium on an order whose casuistry and influence has been prejudicial to morality and the stability of the state.

A distinguished theological professor, who

has been for many years a citizen of Quebec, thus writes on this whole matter :—

"No student of history or observer of the signs of the times, can doubt that the plans of the hierarchy at this moment are most ambitious and comprehensive. The programme of the Vatican and the Jesuits is the capture of Britain and America and through them the subjugation of the whole world. Nor is it spiritual subjugation that is aimed at, but temporal as well. This has always been the doctrine of the church, and it is being propagated of late with unusual boldness in Quebec. *La Vérité*, the strongest of our Ultramontane journals, asserts it with authority. In its issue of the 31st December last, it says, 'the church is not only absolutely independent of the state, but, what is more, superior to it.' Is this claim to be acknowledged throughout our country ? Certainly not. Romanism as a religious and political system—we cannot separate the two factors, they are thoroughly interwoven—is to be resisted to the utmost. If we are asked why ? We answer, in brief, because it perverts and suppresses the truth of God—is now in the main Jesuitism—corrupts and poisons the fountains of education, elementary and advanced—makes national education and national unity in Canada on a true basis impossible—cripples human freedom and undeniably impoverishes the people. The Bible is interdicted and has been burned at the instance of Rome in this province. Her schools are hotbeds of superstition, in which pupils waste their time over vapid legends of the saints, and are obliged to degrade and sacrifice their manhood in the confessional. The vast majority of the people are made poor and non-progressive by the unlimited exactions of the church. They are not free in any true sense; but the spirit of liberty is rising in their breasts, and all true patriots should help them to cast off the yoke. It is not too much to look for the downfall of Romanism. That which it hates and fears most—the Word of the living God—is the appointed instrument of its overthrow. Let us, therefore, speedily give it to all; and in this terrible battle with error, which is daily increasing in magnitude, let us, with the faith of the heroic Carey, 'expect great things *from* God, and attempt great things *for* God.'" *

---

* Rev. Principal MacVicar.

ENGLAND'S VICTORY OVER THE ARMADA.

The malign effects of educating priests in foreign and Romish countries.

In the sixteenth century seminaries and colleges were founded in Spain, France and Italy by English Catholics for educating young Catholics for the functions of the priesthood in England. From these institutions came those swarms of Jesuits and seminary priests which, in the middle of Queen Elizabeth's reign, filled England with conspiracies and treason, aiming at nothing less than the life of the queen and the overthrow of the country. Canadians should observe that in this year of grace a Canadian college has been opened in Rome " to educate young Canadian Catholics according to the Catholic theology, for the administration of priestly functions." From Canadians so educated this country has nothing better to expect, under similar circumstances, than sprang from the same source to the Mother Country three hundred years ago. The foreign training in mediæval doctrines, in the Jesuitical and priestly arts, in dislike of English liberty and history, and antagonism to Protestant freedom and intelligence, renders them anything but an acquisition to Canada. They will return full of devotion to a foreign church, an ancient hier-

Its results in England.

Must be hurtful to Canada.

archy, absolute ecclesiastical power, the chair of St. Peter, and the thunderer of the Vatican.

Romanism cherishes foreign, ancient and obsolete religious notions.

Romanism is still inspired by the same principles and spirit of intolerance, cherishes the same schemes, and pursues the same ends as of old. Her dominance in Canada will be blight, and debasement to Canada worse than was that of Philip the Second and Sextus the Fifth over Spain. Her aim is to tamper with, and, if possible, control education. If it cannot be

She has no sympathy with generous and liberal ideas and progress.

altogether according to her model, to approximate it as closely as possible. She aims to mould the young—young Protestants as well as Catholics. To this end she has her camps of instruction—cheap schools and colleges—under the suasive instruction of monks and nuns, novitiates and priests. These drill mas-

She educates the young, not in the ideals of the present, but the past.

ters teach their recruits to respect the triple tiara more than the royal crown, the Church of Rome more than the Saviour of men, rites and ceremonies more than the oracles of God.

The need of being aroused from our apathy.

Would that we all might be aroused from our apathy on these matters and that each of us feeling himself responsible for liege service to Christ and the best interests of our fellow-men, would promptly come forth "to the help of the Lord, to the help of the Lord against the mighty." Four years or so ago the news spread over the eastern parts of this Dominion that insurrection and rebellion had broken out in the North-West, and were doing and threatening to do a work of destruction on the property and lives of the settlers in those parts. Immediately a spirit of resistance and repression was aroused. Companies, battalions and regiments of brave volunteers offered themselves to go and quell the tumult and restore order. An adequate army was organized, which in a few months returned clothed with honour, having successfully accomplished in that short time the patriotic task they volunteered to perform.

How speedily our volunteers responded to the emergency and suppressed insurrection and rebellion in the North-West!

Would that such a regard for the integrity and stability of our free Christian institutions, our cherished traditional rights, the cause of Christ and the good of our fellow-citizens, animated all classes and divisions of our Reformed and Protestant countrymen! Would that they were one in sentiment and spirit, to boldly meet and heroically oppose every invasion of their dear-bought and priceless inheritance! We want them to be men

The spirit of loyalty and devotion to the truth and to the interests and rights we inherit needed.

of courage and of faith, men of purpose and of power, "men of skill who can keep rank, and are not of double heart!"

"When Spain and Rome their force united
    To crush out freedom's cause,
Our fathers rallied for the right
    And honour of our laws;
Both round the throne and altar,
    And home's sweet sheltering tree,
These gallant sons of old contended;
    And so, true hearts, will we.

"We want not triumphs sprung from force,
    They stain the noblest cause;
For not in might or blood does truth
    Inscribe her perfect laws.
Our spears and swords are printed words,
    The mind our battle-plain;
We've won such victories before,
    And so we can again.

"This makes us stand the foremost
    Among the brave and free;
Our gallant sires of old contended,
    And so, true hearts, will we."

www.ingramcontent.com/pod-product-compliance
Lightning Source LLC
Chambersburg PA
CBHW031747230426
43669CB00007B/529